MAKING
THE CASE

INTENTIONAL FATHER ENGAGEMENT

Written By:

David A. Jones

MAKING THE CASE
INTENTIONAL FATHER ENGAGEMENT

Written By: David A. Jones
Edited By: David & Meka Jones
Cover Design: Aaron C. Butler

ISBN: 9781967082629 (Paperback)
ISBN: 9781967082636 (eBook)
ISBN: 9781967082704 (Hardcover)
Library of Congress Control Number: 2025921599

Printed in the United States of America

BookButler Publishing Company
Upper Marlboro, MD 20774

TheBookButler.com

James Way Consulting FatheringMe901.com

Dedication

I dedicate this book first and foremost to my sons (David Jr., Corey, and Bryce), who helped me understand how to skillfully navigate the fatherhood journey. And to my wife, Meka, who has not only been my muse, but she has also been steadfast in ensuring that I complete this project. I thank you, and I love you.

About the Author

David A. Jones, MSW, LMSW - Holds a Bachelor of Arts Degree in Forensic Psychology from John Jay College and a Master of Social Work from Hunter College, City University of New York. He completed a postgraduate clinical institute in Infant Toddler Psychotherapy at the Jewish Board of Children and Family Services. David is a 2016 UCLA Head Start Management Fellow, A 2018 Nike Starting Block Leadership Fellow, and in 2024, he successfully completed the 21st Century Government Innovation Program. He draws upon his experience, clinical skills, and passion for serving others to ensure he stays on the cutting edge of best practice. He was awarded a William Randolph Hearst Foundation fellowship in 2001, and in 2005, The Visiting Nurse Association of America selected him as Innovator of the Year for his outstanding work with fathers.

Table of Contents

FOREWORD

It is insightful…. innovating…inspirational!

Making the Case: Intentional Father Engagement takes you on a journey that brings together the theory, practice, and reality of building a father engagement program.

David Jones has surfaced a much-needed resource because he knows that fathers' roles in their children's lives are powerful drivers of healthy development. Recent studies have shown that engaged fathers contribute to stronger cognitive skills, emotional security, and long-term well-being, while also shaping children's confidence and social relationships. Current research underscores that father engagement is influenced not only by time spent but also by the quality of interactions, fathers' confidence, and the support they receive in balancing work, family, and stress (Cabrera, Volling, & Barr, 2018; Lamb, 2010; Sarkadi, Kristiansson, Oberklaid, & Bremberg, 2008; U.S. Department of Health & Human Services, 2019; BMC Psychology, 2024; Children, 2023; Lidsen, 2024; WBRO, 2025).

The author creates a tapestry that is a symphony of threads, each unique yet essential, coming together to reveal the full value of fathers in the lives of their infants, toddlers, and preschoolers. Beginning with a glimpse into his life, it explodes into a resource for building a father engagement program rich with stories and messages from colleagues, experts, and fathers. Be careful... don't skip a page; you might miss a valuable nugget, as they are peppered throughout the entire book in abundance.

Jones' social work background looms large as he tenderly reveals, in some ways, what is missing in work with fathers, and in others, what is needed with grit and gravitas. It is stated quite clearly in his book. He is told on several occasions, "The reason we like you is because you keep it real with us." And that is what the book does, he keeps it real! And just when you think Jones has left it 'all on the field,' he draws on his poetic prowess and graces the reader with poetry.

As a colleague who was involved in the fatherhood work at the height of its time in Head Start, *Making the Case: Intentional Father Engagement* is a resource that not only provides an evidence-based model for developing a father engagement program, but it also provides the requisite principles and the practicality of the work. It truly emanates life well-lived in the support of fathers in the lives of their children.

Jacquie Davis

Master's in public health

PREFACE

"He will turn the hearts of fathers to their children."
Malachi 4:6

It is my sincere hope that this book, about many of my experiences pondering, planning, and designing services in support of father engagement, fathering practices, and the things that staff working in any organization, but particularly within the Early Childhood Education field can benefit from knowing, understanding, and take into consideration when making the decision to service and support fathers in their parenting practices. It has the potential to become a much-needed resource for practitioners. This has been an interesting journey, to say the least, one that has changed me in so many ways. It is in understanding how I have changed and how the individuals I came to know benefited from our union, and the subsequent impacts, that I write this book.

On behalf of every man who stands up daily or attempts to stand up daily to appreciate, care for, embrace, love, protect, nurture, and provide for their children and families, I am humbled and proud of your consistent tenacity. And on behalf of every woman who has carried the torch patiently waiting for men, some broken, and others in compromised positions, to assume their role and responsibility, I thank you and salute you for holding it down.

I consider myself to be one of the most fortunate individuals in the world. By God's grace, I was able to pay attention to and be concerned about what happens to children when parents are incapable of, or do not, parent responsibly. Some of this is by circumstance, and some by choice. We will never know all the reasons or fully understand why God places us in certain situations, or why I was able to focus on the plight of children, the role fathers play within the family, or the challenges families can and often do face when fathers are not present in a positive way.

Contrary to widespread belief, I did not buy into the media's view of minority men and the perception that they were not concerned for their offspring. More importantly, I found myself challenging those beliefs, stereotypes if you will, in an attempt to dissect the problem further. My research proved meaningful because, based on my initial hypothesis, I found that it was not a lack of care or concern but rather a lack of knowledge and competence that prevented these men from stepping up and taking responsibility for their children.

What I found, contrary to widely held belief, was that much of the research at the time had not even been conducted on the population everyone so frequently talked about, which was not accidental. Understanding this conundrum, I was careful about how I shared my lens and perspective as I prepared for potential backlash.

Spectators rarely, if ever, understand what visionaries do in their laboratories. What is not seen or rarely thought of is the number of hours they labored and toiled. The challenges, frustrations, mistakes, and yet, for some reason, they persisted. The finished project or results never fully tell the story of when they shifted their initial position, second-guessed themselves, painstakingly fought the urge to give up or to quit, and then suddenly, a breakthrough.

This was the justification, the rationale for staying on course and believing that they were truly on to something. And though filled with doubt, they were courageous enough to take the risk by sharing their perspective with others.

I will cover this in greater detail later in the book; however, in January of 1998, I found myself at a national conference in Washington, D.C., presenting on "The Lack of African American Male Involvement in Family Support Programs." This was a long title, and I remember fighting with myself about changing it, attempting to shorten it, and yet this is what I ended up with. The discussion, however, centered on absent fatherhood, which had recently begun to garner significant interest among many, especially in popular media.

At the time, it seemed to me the goal was to find a scapegoat, someone to blame for challenges within the family. The Moynihan Report, officially titled "The Negro Family: The Case for National Action," was a 1965 government report authored by Daniel Patrick Moynihan.

It argued that the high rate of Black single-parent households, particularly those headed by women, was a major impediment to social and economic progress for African Americans and contributed to cycles of poverty. The report's controversial findings sparked intense debate and influenced policy decisions for decades. Understanding this, I thought to myself, *'baby steps.'*

As an actively involved, African American father of young sons, I could speak to the issues I faced and those of other people I knew in the Black community, and yet, I was not confident enough to speak on how these issues, which I felt were universal, impacted other communities. The presentation centered on a discussion of African American Fathers based upon a few critical points.

- The Importance of Fathers

- The History of African American Family Separation

- Obstacles to Father Involvement in the Family

- Suggested program approaches, interventions, and strategies

 This was the on-ramp to aspects of the story that had not been told. In life, the strong become the weak in unfamiliar terrain. They must learn to navigate a set of rules and principles that are foreign to them. When and if they can do so, survival is within their grasp. If they cannot find a way to do so, they perish. For men, African American men in particular, to fully understand what is expected of them, for them to respond accordingly, and still maintain some sense of self-efficacy over their world, their universe, there not only has to be individual changes in how they view and navigate the world, but the world must also change in response to their being intentionally different.

Self-efficacy is realized when an opportunity presents itself, and there is fertile ground for fathers to navigate. What this looks like is finding comfort in the notion that you can love your partner and your children, be emotional, care for, and provide for your family, and not be afraid to become increasingly comfortable with vulnerability. And be okay knowing that you can not only feel, but also be hurt.

The years I spent outreaching, recruiting, and engaging men, young and old, to participate in programming geared towards learning about what was important to them, their experiences, and the desires they held for their children, placed me in a unique position.

The question that comes to mind is, will we attempt to win the battle, or should our focus be on the war? Many fathers who attempted to subscribe to the societal definition of being a financial provider were stuck on stupid, trying to live up to a standard for which society failed to properly position them for success in the role. For those of you who are parents, or who have been fortunate to find yourselves in a parenting role, from pregnancy to birth, and then parenting through the various stages, there are levels of complexity where your position, juxtaposed to your child/children, shifts constantly.

Today, my life is filled with rich experiences because of this important work. I have met, interacted with, and come to know many great men. Men who the world had given up on, written off, men who defied the odds, finding a way to embrace a new role and new responsibilities. My experiences have given me the opportunity to develop a universal message that has been embraced by many: fathers matter!

I reflect on the complexity of the fathering role, and yes, the simplicity embedded within it, which starts with just being present, then being fully present, then scaffolding one's knowledge, then being able to constantly pivot and shift, and then waking up the next day to do it all over again. I did not have a foundation for program implementation; all I had was a basic understanding of the totality of my experiences at the time. However, when one starts a new program, they are tasked with a tremendous responsibility.

The goal of course is to develop programming that addresses an identified need and delivers proven outcomes resulting in sustained, positive change. To design a service that is considerate and respectful of the client population, with the capacity to decipher and respond to challenges that may inhibit the overall objective. Finally, it means being able to deliver the goods in a way that can be replicated. Or maybe not for every program, as every situation is unique within itself. What I can say with confidence is that the Fathers First and The Bronx Fatherhood programs were designed to do what we intended.

My team and I found a way to help men decipher for themselves how they could define the fathering role, no longer attempting to live up to a standard based on others' preconceived notions of what fathering should be or look like. We helped them move from a place of ignorance, which does not mean stupid, but more so a lack of knowledge and insight, to a place of increased competence.

I have always believed that, for most people, confidence increases with competence. When this happens, individuals can put into practice, even if only at a basic level, what they have learned. Sound fathering is a process within itself, of constant learning, constant adjustment, constant self-modulation, self-regulation, and self-reflection.

Questions and doubt fill every act when one is genuinely interested in getting it right. The question that always remains is how decisions, encounters, and interactions fathers have with their children impact who they eventually become. I have several sons, and they are distinctly unique individuals. I have found a way to develop and balance significant individual relationships with each of them. I pride myself on being able to appropriately balance our relationships where the expectations are clear, and mutual respect is in proper order. This is because, now that they are young adults, my role is more of an advisor, counselor, and coach. The foundation for this relationship was built when they were young.

I know, based on my experiences, that you can find that sweet spot. If one is able to establish the right relationship with their children, the potential is unlimited. And while the pressure is immense, I would imagine that most, if not all, parents at some point grapple with questions of ability and competency in their quest to get it right. When I ventured out, whether it was a national conference or a localized training, I'd caution practitioners in attendance as they moved through the workshops and/or conversations, prompting them to ponder their own motivations for this work. It was important for them to remember that teaching parenting skills has a greater impact when parents are able to interact with their children.

Many fathers we meet in the context of this work are separated from their children. They have limited opportunities to interact with their child until we, the professionals, who yield a certain amount of power over their lives, vouch for them and say they have accomplished or met a specific goal. Fatherhood and good parenting do not need to look a certain way for us to validate or cosign on their progress.

There are so many aspects of parenting, the way in which parents, in particular fathers, feel about their child that we are not privy to and will never see. Holding a child in your mind is an invisible parenting act. The emotion one feels when they interact with and/or embrace their child is visible, yet subjective. Taking a child to school every day is a luxury not afforded to everyone.

Understanding the importance of developing a relationship with teachers to ensure your child is learning and growing is a parenting act. Understanding that conflict is an innate component of all relationships, and that helping our children navigate it is an important part of parenting, is why communication and fostering a healthy parenting relationship with the child's mother, whether cohabitating or not, are essential.

My team and I typically left our training sessions feeling optimistic and hopeful based on the feedback we received. We could usually tell when we had been impactful. Participants walked away with additional information and vowed to be intentionally different in the places and spaces where they had opportunities to interact with and engage fathers.

On the heels of several presentations, satisfied attendees shared that they appreciate my content, experience, and facilitation. Then they share, while all of this is great, we cannot clone you, package you, and take you everywhere. So, what is it that we can do, and how can we draw upon your knowledge, expertise, and skill to be as impactful?

When I reflect on my experiences, I am in awe of what they see, because I do not think I possess skills that are different than those of my well-intentioned colleagues and other practitioners, who are committed to succeeding in this important work. I tried to be authentically me in the days, hours, minutes, and moments I spent with fathers and staff who were interested in supporting them. I am usually locked in, trying to make a connection, listening intently to what fathers are saying, not sharing, and desperately trying to reply to them, often asking questions to help them think and gain insight into their personal situation.

The question becomes: how can practitioners be more impactful, and how can they help fathers develop the capacity to increase their competency in caring for their children? An important question for us to consider is: what are we really referring to when we say we want to make an impact or be impactful? One way to define impact is to have a powerful effect on a situation or a person.

Within this context, I reference it to mean having someone be intentionally different after an encounter, or a series of encounters, resulting in a pivotal change in attitude, thoughts, and behaviors, culminating in lasting and sustainable change. This book will help practitioners explore and gain insight into the parallel process of fathers' development as they evolve as men while responding to and embracing their role, navigating life, and their parenting responsibilities.

Part I

Helping Fathers - Chasing Dreams

"The stone that the builder refused is going to
be the cornerstone!"
Psalm 118:22

This is my story as only I can tell it. In all actuality, I cannot really say if this is a story that has meaning for anyone other than myself. What I can say is I have had the great fortune to be able to learn some things in life that I can share with others in a way that might make a difference. I listened to God's anointing over my life, resulting in a ride that has amazed me in some instances, shocked me on occasions, and even scared me in others.

Obedience is funny in that, most often, when we think we are being obedient, we are not. A true understanding of what it means to be obedient is when we can stop, listen, watch, wait, and finally adapt. The question becomes, what voice are we listening to? Are we even aware? Is it our inner voice responding to instinctual influence? Are we truly acting upon God's word? What does it mean to be anointed or have an ordination to do something? An anointing signifies divine empowerment, consecration, and favor bestowed by the holy spirit, enabling individuals to fulfill a specific purpose or calling.

Purposes or callings are viewed, by many, as sources of strength, enabling individuals to accomplish tasks they might not be able to do on their own. In the end, it symbolizes God's favor, protection, and presence of His spirit, ensuring success in endeavors. An ordination or being ordained to do a particular thing means being appointed or set apart by God for a specific purpose or role, often within a religious context, which is why so many people would say to me that I was doing God's work!

Adults make decisions all the time without thinking about the consequences. Even if they are throwing caution to the wind as it relates to their own life, what about their children? What is interesting to me is that I grew up poor, and like so many other poor folks from my generation, I did not have a clue.

There were signs, things that should be on the shoulders of adults that fell on the radar of me and my siblings. And even when we thought we were aware or understood, we really did not. Our young brains could not fully comprehend the magnitude of what we were witnessing or hearing. It was not until I observed how friends and neighbors lived their lives, embracing societal norms and modeling what was acceptable and what was not, that I began to understand the chasm between the haves and the have-nots.

Growing up poor provides one with perspective. It is good when you have, but when you do not, you just make do, make believe, or make a way. What do I mean by make do? You accept the fact that at this moment in time, my wants are not a priority. So, I might have to eat peanut butter without jelly and be damn happy that I can.

Making believe is easy when your basic necessities are not always readily available; you improvise or pretend. Or, if I choose to make a way, I have to settle for preserves as a substitute for jelly, which I would not prefer, and yet, in the moment, it will have to do.

There is a word researchers often use to try to define and measure, to my astonishment, how individuals overcome difficult situations. The goal is to try and understand how someone who has gone through these challenging situations demonstrates the ability not only to navigate them but also to survive and, in some instances, surpass expectations. Resilience is the word I am referring to, which is used loosely to describe an innate ability in some individuals to survive when the odds are stacked against them.

I found myself listening to that inner voice, which I quickly realized was God placing things in my vision for me to see, be curious, and/or care about, without a clear understanding of what was expected of me or how I would accomplish the tasks. I responded with the best intentions because I did not have a clue about what I was doing. Were they the right things? How was it possible, then, that the fatherless became someone who helped so many others navigate this developmental trajectory we call fatherhood?

This is biblical, and we've seen it many times before: the fatherless fathering themselves and helping others father not only themselves but also their children. This is my story!

Growing up without my father actively engaged in my life was not a big thing. Losing my mom at the age of ten was devastating. I did not immediately feel the impact of not having a father. I am sure economically, my life could have been better in some ways, and some of those essential early life lessons that are so meaningful, related to thinking about and planning out my future from the perspective of a male role model, were absent.

And yet, because I did have worthy substitutes, uncles, and older cousins, I was good. Losing my mother was another story altogether. She was my lifeline and the individual whom I loved and looked up to for everything. Every significant life lesson I had learned up to this point was taught to me by her, her friends, or family members, and now she was gone.

Throughout this story, one interesting thing about my journey was the totality of my experiences, which prepared me to tap into resilience and a faith that seemed unwavering. I was born and raised in New York City, so I learned a lot about how to navigate life at an early age. I had to make sense of it all. My early education was compromised because my mom was not home a lot because she worked two jobs, and then she became ill. I was so focused and concerned about her well-being and the thought of losing the most important individual in my life to cancer that I had difficulty focusing and attuning in elementary school. Couple that with the fact that there was such devastation and violence in my community.

You see, I was not more than 7 or 8 years old when I had to step over a dead junkie's body to get out of my building one morning on Fox Street on the way to school. In the summer, I witnessed gang fights, turf wars where neighbors, people that I knew, were stabbed and beaten unconscious. Others were kicked, hit in the head with bottles, and afterwards they were rushed away to Lincoln Hospital by ambulance. The interesting thing is that there was so much diversity on my block in the South Bronx; I likened my neighborhood to a mini–United Nations. For the most part, people got along. My apartment building was filled with rich culture. I can still remember the smells of the different foods emanating from apartments adjacent to ours. And yet, the violence in our community was normalized. This was my home, and it prepared me for how to skillfully navigate dangerous environments. After my mother's death, my siblings and I moved to Georgia to live with my maternal grandmother.

We went from a single-parent home to a village of family members: aunts, uncles, older cousins, and more family than I could count at the time. It felt like we were related to everyone we met. The thing that I believe impacted me the most was adapting to the remnants of segregation. Everything was divided by the proverbial color line, even though segregation had ended. The laws changed, and schools were supposed to desegregate. The community where we lived was filled with so much racial hate, and there were challenges my family members and I experienced when transitioning into the White schools.

It was 1973, and White children and some adults threw Coca-Cola bottles at the school bus when it pulled into the parking lot. As a 10-year-old, I remember seeing those infamous colored and white-water fountains. I was not able to sit at the counter at Taylor's drug store in Waynesboro, one of the only places that would serve colored's, which is how White folks referred to us back then. I remember going to that drug store on a couple of occasions, having to enter through the back door.

What was fascinating to me, years later, when I walked into that same drug store with my school's letterman jacket on, the staff welcomed, encouraged, celebrated, and even admonished me about winning a ball game. This was another pivotal adjustment that prepared me for situations I would experience later in life. There were so many lessons I learned after moving to Alexander, Georgia. I learned about the history of the one-room schoolhouse in the slave quarters, where many of my family members went to school. During segregation, African American educators held a unique role teaching children in their community in the face of immense challenges, danger, and with limited resources.

They worked tirelessly to build schools and provide quality education, despite facing discrimination, prejudice, and threats. They played a pivotal role in the lives of Black students, often serving as mentors and role models. Segregated schools were often underfunded and lacked resources compared to White schools. Racial barriers limited the career options available to Black educators, with many choosing teaching to empower their communities. These Black educators took a holistic approach, emphasizing not only academic learning but also a sense of civic responsibility, encouraging us to be active participants in the fight for equality.

As mentors and role models, they instilled a sense of pride and self-worth in Black students because they had little hope for their future. They advocated for equality and justice, and their dedication and hard work laid the foundation for future educational advancements.

Although they faced many challenges during segregation, African American educators played a critical role in shaping their students' lives and in the broader struggle for civil rights and educational equality. Their dedication and resilience continue to inspire educators and students today.

It is hard to believe that, after growing up and living in New York, immersed in an ethnically diverse culture that appreciated our shared values, I was now in the deep South, in an environment consumed with hate, where the focus was on our differences. In New York, I learned to navigate city streets and adjacent neighborhoods, and to use the city's sophisticated subway system, while learning to speak Spanish. Leaving New York meant I would not be able to continue some of the extracurricular activities I enjoyed. I had to give up my music lessons. I was learning to play the Viola, and I had taken class trips to Radio City and Carnegie Hall. Students who had promise were told that if they practiced their craft, they might end up playing at these venues one day. I was getting surprisingly good at it and had been told by my teacher that I had a future in music. Once I entered the Georgia school system, I never picked up an instrument again.

Even with my compromised early educational experience, I was a smart child. I was placed in the top classes in each grade from seventh through twelfth. I graduated early in my senior year. I never really acclimated to school in Georgia. I did not like it there, and I did not feel like I ever really belonged, so true adaptation was not possible. I did not like the teachers or their approach to supporting students. I realized early on that they did not have my best interest at heart with respect to what they taught and how the information was shared. I also had difficulty with the guidance the school counselor provided. The Georgia school system's goal was structured to create employees, field hands, farmers, and factory workers. I was not interested in any of those vocations. I made the best of the situation, developed relationships with a few friends, played on several school teams, and graduated ahead of schedule. I am not sure why, but I had a burning desire to leave there on the first thing smoking. I missed New York terribly and was focused on positioning myself so I could get back.

My experience in the Georgia education system turned me against school, and I graduated believing I was not capable of navigating college successfully. My only outlet was following in my older brother's footsteps, so I joined the Air Force. Had I truly had my head on a swivel at the time, I would have realized that I had to be smart to get into the Air Force, the branch of the military that requires, at least in my mind, a higher level of academic prowess and intellect. My experience there benefited me in ways I might discuss later; however, I quickly learned that I was an independent thinker. That is, groupthink and following the directions of others who did not seem more competent than I was did not work for me.

I also had difficulty with mind games and abuse of authority. Reflecting on that time now, I was not mature enough to skillfully leverage the situation to my advantage, and I joined the Air Force for all the wrong reasons. My goal was to get away from Georgia. My dissatisfaction with my decision resulted in my making mistakes. My character of service was solid, I was good at my job, and I received a couple of commendations, which is what saved me. It was situations I encountered when I was not working that eventually put me in the line of fire, resulting in a circumstance that ended with my being honorably discharged. Needless to say, it initially felt like a failure. Although it took a while, I was able to realize a military career was not what God had planned for my life. And yet, somewhere in the recesses of my mind, it still felt like a failure, so I began taking steps to order my life so that I would never fail at anything I chose to do again.

When I left for the military, in addition to desperately wanting to get away, I was going to show everyone. I wanted my family and the few friends I had made to see that I could make it. I wanted them to see that I could make it in another part of the world. Truthfully, these self-declarations were things I had conjured up in my head. These were thoughts that only mattered to me. After all, it was my life, right? No one else really cared that much.

However, as one might imagine, coming back home was difficult. I did not want to leave the house; I did not want to see anyone, and I did not have a plan for my next steps. What was worse, I was back in a place where I did not want to be, and I had no idea how I was going to get out. I think the first time I saw the quote, "There is opportunity in every crisis," I could not fully embrace it. To be honest, it is hard for most of us to move beyond the crisis and see and fully embrace the opportunities that result.

My departure from Georgia was on the heels of a minor crisis, which quickly let me know that I would never be able to survive as an adult Black male who was an independent thinker with ideas of his own in the deep south, so I returned to New York. The interesting thing about my return was that NY felt both different and familiar at the same time, which meant I still loved the fast pace and energy. However, I was now living on West End Avenue, 65th Street, instead of in the South Bronx. I was living amongst the Manhattan elite.

Noteworthy progress had been made. In my observation, the pace of the city that never sleeps has accelerated. I felt in my gut that I was back home where I belonged. I was excited about the possibilities and was confident that I would eventually find my way.

Discovering Head Start

"Engagement is not just about how we move in;
it's also about how long we stay"
(D. Jones)

In 1995, my life changed in a way I could never have imagined. A friend and former colleague I met while working at St. Luke's Roosevelt Hospital's Second Chance program called to share good news and some challenging news. The good news was that she was getting married and inviting me to the wedding. Her fiancé was getting a transfer to Atlanta, Georgia, so she would be leaving New York with him right after the wedding.

The more challenging news was that she would have to leave her current job as Director of a new program she had just gotten underway. It was an Early Childhood Education program in Far Rockaway, Queens. She had promised her supervisor before she left that she would identify someone who could step into her role to lead and implement this new program. I did not know much about early childhood education at the time. Although I had become a father with children of my own, my experience and outlook remained quite limited. To be honest, I was reluctant but curious, so I promised her that if she sent me the information, I would review it and at least consider the offer.

Andrea and I worked together at the Second Change Program, so she knew my work ethic. We were not only colleagues; we were also friends, and we had a shared interest in social work. I had solicited her advice when I decided to pursue a degree in Social Work.

She had graduated from Columbia University, so of course, she was trying to encourage me to apply. I was more interested in attending Hunter College because I thought I would have a better chance of being accepted. I did not think I was Columbia material, and at the time, Hunter College School of Social Work was the top-rated school in the country. They also had a One-Year Residency Program for adults already working in the field, which I was interested in learning more about. Finally, we were both passionate about working with and supporting adolescents in their transition to adulthood.

Everything was happening fast. As promised, I reviewed the content she had sent, and before I knew it, I was having a preliminary telephone conversation with her supervisor. The conversation was successful, so I was invited for an interview. I put on a nice blue suit, Stacy Adam shoes, and I was out the door. I walked into 1250 Broadway, the Manhattan office of the Visiting Nurse Service of New York, to meet with a woman named Priscilla Lincoln. This visit marked the beginning of subsequent trips to the building. I would eventually have an office in that very same building. Priscilla was a Maternal Child Health nurse with extensive experience overseeing all Maternal Child Health Programs. We met, had an interview that was more like a conversation to be truthful, and I walked out feeling confident.

Prior to leaving, she directed me to the Human Resources office, where I met with one of the managers, Helen Merchan, to complete a formal application. About thirty minutes later, I left the building a little excited and nervous. I was almost certain that the job was mine, but then again, I was not sure. I received confirmation later that week, and again I was happy, a little surprised, and somewhat shocked that I'd actually been chosen.

This was going to be a lot of work and a huge learning curve. It would also be a wonderful opportunity to do something meaningful for a community with significant needs. However, this would not be my first rodeo with Far Rockway.

Andrea left the hospital before I did. She called a few months later and asked me to help her with the In-Step program. It was a program for pregnant & parenting teens, funded by the National Organization for Adolescent Parenting Prevention, now known as the Healthy Teen Network. My task was to provide outreach to adolescent fathers and attempt to get them positively involved in the program. Because this was a new initiative, an expanded service, I had to create a process for conducting community outreach.

Community Outreach is interesting work, and I quickly came to realize that when developing a structured approach to this kind of work, you fake it until you make it. Working in underserved communities enhances one's observational skills and awareness. It enables you to identify and learn where potential community resources are located. If one is astute, one begins to learn about and almost feel the heartbeat of the community. The Far Rockaway peninsula was eleven miles long and three miles wide, with the ocean and bay as borders.

There are areas that are safe and areas where one needs to proceed with extreme caution. There were at least seven different housing developments, a couple in particular; Redfern, the Forty's housing project, Hammels, and Edgemere were the worst developments in New York City as it relates to poverty, drugs, gangs, and gang violence. As a service provider at best, you are an interloper in unfamiliar territory, and the natives have no problem letting you know you do not belong. That is until they discover that you come in peace and that you do not mean them or their business any harm.

At first, I did not like doing outreach in the housing developments. To be honest, many were not safe. The elevators did not always work, stairwells were dark and smelled of urine, and street pharmacists were actively conducting business. I had to adjust to watching transactions unfold right before my eyes, which at any moment could escalate into a violent situation.

Funny, this is where those early experiences, as a child growing up in the Bronx, served me well. Yes, what they were doing was not legal, and no, it was not any of my business. It was not my place to report what they were doing to anyone. I wisely pretended not to see these transactions and the frequent violence accompanying them. To add to the element of potential danger, when I was able to meet with a father at home, I witnessed disinterest in my conversations and the services I offered. The encounters were rushed, and on more than one occasion, I was politely ushered out the door.

For some people in my position, this would have been a deterrent. However, it became a personal challenge. Fatherhood, being a part of their child's life, did not seem like a priority, or if it was, it was not the main priority. They regarded their challenges in interacting with their child's mother as a major obstacle. Several of these young men, talented in athletics, focused more on their futures in football or basketball and did not fully grasp the responsibilities before them.

In the beginning, it was hard to get these young men to focus on what was in the best interest of their child, how important it was for them to be actively engaged in their child's development, as well as how important it would be for them to establish, maintain, and sustain a healthy co-parenting relationship with their children's mother.

Over time, the community, including the street pharmacists, recognizing that I was not a threat, welcomed me. I would get a "what's up?" Or a high five and sometimes a cautionary look, alerting me not to walk into a building or down a particular block. However, I was now safe. After building trust with several of the young fathers, I was able to start weekly parenting education groups. The majority of studies examining men's roles as fathers have focused primarily on White, middle-class fathers, addressing their specific concerns and identifying perceived obstacles to maintaining active, healthy engagement in their children's lives.

It seems somewhat inappropriate for me to judge; however, compared to these young fathers, they didn't have real challenges fathering their children; they had work-life balance issues, they had time commitment issues, and they, too, seemed to be having difficulty prioritizing their children, although they articulated that they wanted better communication and stronger connections with them. I immediately recognized that I had to tailor my conversations to make them culturally relevant to the young Black and Latino men sitting in front of me.

I connected best-practice research and parenting information to relevant conversations, topics, and experiences that fathers could relate to and apply to their daily lives. Making the educational content relevant in this way helped them not only connect with and understand but also appreciate what they were learning, because they saw themselves and their circumstances in the conversations, group discussions, stories, and case scenarios. I did not immediately make the connection; however, I was paying homage to those early Black educators.

It was amazing to be able to participate, facilitate, and at the same time witness their engagement. I felt so blessed that I was able to listen to what God had placed on my heart to not only care about and be concerned about young Black and Latino men, but to have an opportunity to do something about their plight was a blessing within itself. Investing in preventive measures in marginalized communities can be so impactful.

Many social service programs are geared to intervene after a situation has evolved to the problem stage. And yes, it is true that Early Steps was an intervention program; however, I provided outreach and educational support to enrolled fathers and young men who were not yet fathers.

They walked away with timely, relevant information they could draw upon later in life. Of course, as life would have it, just as we were beginning to gain real traction and start making an impact, there was an issue with the funding, and my contracted position ended. As I reflect now, what was interesting was how I grew in my understanding of the work and my ability to make important connections about how to do it the right way. I was laser-focused on authenticity, honesty, and integrity; essential competencies needed to provide direct service that contributes to meaningful outcomes for the fathers.

Authenticity made me relatable because, in some instances, I was painfully honest, and the fathers appreciated it. They often shared, *"The reason we like you is because you keep it real with us."* Having integrity in our work enables us to constantly self-assess to ensure the focus is on the client's needs, rather than our own. This approach ensured the work was about the strategies I used, however it was not about me, or benefiting me more than the young fathers who allowed me to enter their lives, sharing knowledge and lending advice. These were the skills that would come in handy in the future.

So, coming back to Far Rockaway to implement Early Head Start was going to provide me with another opportunity. Thankfully, I was able to envision changes and enhanced services that others could not, and to this day, I am not sure how I did it. In my first few weeks, I concentrated on reading the request for proposal. I wanted to understand what it was that we were supposed to be doing. I met with Jean Fitch, the only other staff member hired as part of what would become a much larger team. I spent a great deal of time reading the Head Start Program Performance Standards to gain insight into the compliance expectations.

The Head Start Program Performance Standards proved to be a valuable resource. As far as procedural guidelines go, not only were they a rigorous set of criteria grounded in best practice and solid research, but they were also user-friendly. The focus on continuous program improvement, high-quality, timely, and responsive caregiving, and parent involvement in decision-making led me to develop a philosophical approach to designing and implementing services to enhance families, which has served me quite well to this day. I easily understood some parts, and other aspects of the regulations were foreign. Nevertheless, I tried as best I could to understand. I asked Jean and Priscilla clarifying questions whenever we met. I felt like a fish out of water, yet my supervisor seemed happy with my progress. On this day, I headed into Manhattan to meet with her for supervision.

I was developing a respect for her knowledge and understanding of the task at hand. She always welcomed me, asked questions about my progress, and then assigned me additional tasks. On this occasion, she had good news. She told me I needed to pack a bag because we were going to a full week of training for new directors in Hilton Head, South Carolina.

This came out of nowhere, and although surprised, I was willing. I had only been on the job for a couple of weeks, a little less than a month. Traveling was not an issue for me; however, I would have to leave my family. This would be the longest amount of time I would be away since my children were born. I soon realized, as you will too, that it would be an adjustment I would have to get used to as I would find myself traveling a great deal in the future.

SOUTH CAROLINA

Hilton Head, South Carolina

Hilton Head Island is only twenty miles north of Savannah, Georgia, and 95 miles south of Charleston. It is part of the low country region in South Carolina. The Program for Infant Toddler Caregiver Training was at a resort, a place known for its natural beauty, including pristine beaches and large live oaks covered in moss. It is a beautiful island where nature literally takes center stage. A place for individuals with money to come decompress, pamper themselves, and play a little golf. Had it not been for this Head Start Training, I would not have known about Hilton Head, nor would I have had a desire to visit.

If memory serves me correctly, we flew from New York to Charleston, then we were put on a smaller plane, one I referred to as a crop duster, carrying a maximum of 8 to 12 passengers, and we flew into a small airport near the resort. This was the first time I felt unsafe during a flight. The plane's engine was extremely loud, reminding me of a lawnmower engine, and it seemed as if you could feel every maneuver the pilot made.

Thank God, we landed safely. We arrived at the property, and as expected, it was magical. The Oaks stood tall, piercing the sky, the landscape was well-manicured, and what was even more astonishing were the alligators roaming the grounds. I learned that the community was a 600-acre natural habitat for wildlife. Signs were near the entrance of the hotel warning guests to be aware that alligators were on the property.

I checked in without incident and went to my room. It was nice, well-manicured, and everything was in its proper place. But the solitude was even better, oh my goodness, the solitude was delightful.

No one is calling my name, asking me to give them something or take them somewhere. I had time to myself, to focus and to think. I wondered if all of the rooms were this nice. At this point, I had not stayed in many hotels, and I have to say this was one of the nicest. I was going to be here for an entire week. Yes, and it was in that moment that I vowed to enjoy this to the fullest. I unpacked and put my things away in what I felt was an organized fashion, then set out to explore. The resort was spacious and had amenities, including a gym, which I was eager to use. And what a gym it was, it had everything, universals, treadmills, ellipticals, free weights, and stationary bikes.

The New York City Wave II - Early Head Start grant recipients held weekly cluster meetings, where I had the opportunity to meet and connect with other staff from agencies implementing similar programs. This was going to make my being here a little easier because I had begun building relationships with a few other people besides Priscilla. I knew quite a few Program Directors and Coordinators. I saw a couple of them checking in as I walked the grounds. We chatted briefly, agreeing to meet at the bar later that evening for a drink. I also saw others enjoying the pool.

I stopped by the registration desk and checked into the conference. I received a handbag with pens, markers, and manipulatives. They gave me a huge binder filled with reading material. This was more material than I had read in my first semester in college. Reading and learning about early childhood knowledge, standards, policies, procedures, and best practices, I quickly realized that reading this type of content was going to be the norm for the next few years.

I walked back to my room to change so I could go to the gym. I hit the Sauna to loosen up, and afterwards, I spent a good 90 minutes in the gym on various machines to the point of exhaustion. My legs felt strong and weak at the same time. I felt refreshed after a hot shower. I wrapped my towel around me after drying off and lay across the bed in my nakedness.

I was not in a hurry to put on any clothes, nor to leave the room. After twenty minutes, I decided to pick out my clothes. I chose a pair of cargo pants, a crisp white short-sleeved shirt, and slipped on a pair of Air Force Ones. It was time to go to the ballroom for lunch, so I decided to walk down early. I ran into Priscilla and Judythe Dim, one of the other directors, talking outside the ballroom. Priscilla smiled as I approached. She dressed casually and looked comfortable. I felt good about my interpretation of the memo she sent about the appropriate attire for this event.

I walked over and said hello, and we made idle chitchat until it was time to take our seats. There were Butlers everywhere, going about their business, serving guests, and ensuring everything was in its proper place.

The table was formerly set, and I was looking at the forks to make sure I would remember to use the right one for my salad. The set-up reminded me of when I first learned appropriate dining etiquette during basic military training. There was a stage, a podium, and several chairs for members of the Program for Infant Toddler Caregiver Team. I later learned these would be the individuals facilitating the content we would be immersing ourselves in during the week.

The keynote speaker, John Ronald Lally, was the Director of WestEd's Center for Child and Family Studies. The training content was based on the seminal work of Magda Gerber, a Hungarian-American early childhood educator known for her "Educaring Philosophy," which emphasized respectful, responsive care for infants and toddlers. Known to all as Ron, he was a pioneer in infant and toddler development and care. He was an enthusiastic champion focused on ensuring that infants, toddlers, and preschool children received quality early childhood education. I could tell by his remarks that all of the descriptions were true.

I felt excited and impassioned to begin the week of training after he concluded his speech. The other members of his team, Peter, Maria, and Doug, introduced themselves, shared a little about their respective backgrounds and the content they would be focusing on throughout the week, and then we began table introductions. As I looked around the room, I noticed that outside of the West Ed Team and a couple of Federal staff, I was one of the few male attendees in the ballroom.

I cannot say for sure, but there must have been at least two hundred plus individuals in the room. At this point in my career, I cannot say I had spoken in front of that many people before, and yet, because of the relaxed atmosphere and the excitement that filled the room, I was not afraid when it came time for me to introduce myself.

I stood up, said my name, and proudly announced that I was the Program Coordinator and that I had been on the job for less than a month. The sound of thunderous applause caught me by surprise. It was at that moment, and at other times during the week, that I realized the magnitude of not only being here but also of my being in such a significant role.

After all of the pomp and circumstance, we had time to enjoy our meal. The servers were busy bringing food and drinks to each table while the attendees began talking amongst themselves. Even though I had introduced myself as a Project Coordinator, it was interesting that many in the room assumed that I was a father, a recipient of Head Start services, and that I came as a parent Policy Council member representing a program. People were surprised that I was responsible for implementing the program, which surprised me a little, and yet I was just taking it in and trying to make sense of it all.

This was the beginning of my week of intensive training at Hilton Head. We were at a beautiful resort with amazing surroundings, yet for the 6 days we were there, we trained from 7:30 in the morning until 6:00 pm. This is what you call an intense institute. I made many connections, met a few new colleagues, and, despite all my learning, walked away excited yet filled with questions.

———————————————

Hiring Staff

Listening for God's Guidance and Grace

I took a couple of days off after returning from Hilton Head to decompress and reconnect. My family responsibilities and the week I had just experienced began to help put things into perspective. I was a leader, a father, an advocate for early childhood education, and now responsible for ensuring that children in Far Rockaway, Queens, would have the same experiences and opportunities that I was attempting to provide for my own children. Faced with what I was beginning to understand was a daunting task, yet I was up for the challenge. The week concluded with Priscilla and I revising our priorities. The assignments she gave me now make so much more sense. I rolled up my sleeves and began to organize and plan for the tasks my team and I needed to complete.

Jean, the nurse, was the Health Coordinator, and although we were in parallel roles, she had reporting responsibility to me. When it was time to review resumes, I asked Jean for her input. I could not immediately place my finger on the problem; however, it was clear that she was having issues with me. I was not sure why; however, it was impacting our communication and our ability to move the work forward.

I later discovered that nurse supervision should be handled by more experienced nurses, which made it uncomfortable for her to report to me about her duties. In addition, I learned that she was either married to or involved with an African American male in the past. They had a couple of children, but he was abusive, and he had abandoned her. Every day when she looked at me, I was a representation of her dreadful past, and she was not only uncomfortable around me, but she was also having difficulty collaborating with me. I did not have the experience or depth of understanding that I do now, so I honestly could not appreciate how difficult this was for her at the time, nor did I care. I was driven; we had a job to do, there were aspects of the work we needed to collaborate on, and I expected her to do her part.

Leadership, project management, and supervision provide us with a wealth of knowledge and opportunities to gain experience if done properly. I have to say, I fumbled this situation badly. We got off to a terrible start because, every time she tried to retreat, I pulled her closer, wanting to have meaningful dialogue. I wanted to hear her thoughts and get her opinion on hiring decisions, but she was unable to provide what I needed.

I did not have patience, strong listening skills, or insight into how giving her time to reflect would enable her to respond accordingly. She needed time to think about my questions and come back to me to share her thoughts; however, I wanted answers right away. Yes, we got off to a dreadful start, and if I could sit down with her today, I would apologize for my lack of understanding about her past trauma and what I represented for her. The naivety of youth.

I had to hire administrative staff, teachers, and home visitors. Helen Merchan, the woman I met on my first day, was my go-to in H.R., and she was amazing. She explained the recruiting, hiring, orientation, and onboarding processes for the staff that would be joining.

Although this organization had a robust H.R. team, this was the first time they had hired educational staff, teachers with these specific early childhood qualifications, so we communicated a great deal, every day, sometimes frequently throughout the day. I would leave my home a little after 6:00 a.m., drive 30 minutes to Far Rockaway, depending on traffic, and open the office. I was the first one there and usually the last one to leave at the end of the day. This was a pattern that I established. My upbringing and military training had prepared me well for leadership, or so I thought. I looked at so many resumes; it made my head spin.

I was dreaming that I had made a couple of horrific hiring decisions, and the results were devastating. I am not sure about other people; however, when I wake from a bad dream, the first thing I do is say, "Thank God it was only a dream." I then try to make sense of the dream and vow not to put myself in a position where it can become a reality.

It was, to say the least, challenging to find qualified staff who wanted to come all the way out to Far Rockaway to work. We advertised in the local newspaper, 'The WAVE,' and we began to get responses. On one occasion, when Jean felt comfortable enough to talk to me, she suggested we focus on hiring locally and proposed we begin by interviewing parent volunteers from the In-Step program. It was in that moment that it dawned on me: although we had only been in the office together once or twice, she was nurse Jean from In-step, the one everyone always talked about.

I liked her suggestion, thought this was a great idea, and what was even better, I was beginning to make progress with her. Within weeks, I hired additional staff and began holding regular individual and weekly team meetings to discuss our work. The program's goal was unique in that our focus was on serving teen parents.

The data from the Community Assessment suggested that this would be a good segment of the population to focus on, and we were innovative in our Service Delivery Model. The structure would consist of a Home-Based option, in collaboration with the NYC Department of Education, where teen mothers and fathers who are doing well academically can bring their child to school with them and place them in on-site childcare while attending classes. Lastly, we would eventually have a center consisting of four infant-toddler classrooms.

Priscilla and I were in the process of securing an appropriate facility for the Center-Based option. On Fridays, when she came to visit or participate in staff development training, we drove around the peninsula looking for an ideal building to renovate.

We eventually settled on another storefront. The Home-Based option would be our primary method of service delivery for a while. This was one of the reasons it was challenging to hire staff, because it would entail delivering early childhood education services in the homes where the teenagers lived. It is important to understand that we were not only providing essential early childhood education services, but were also respectful and supportive, and educated parents about their role as their child's primary teacher.

We were solidifying their role as advocates. These were foreign concepts to them, and many of them could not fully embrace our approach to communicating and engaging with them when every other adult they had encountered since they discovered and revealed that they were pregnant had told them they ruined their lives.

And although we were preparing them for greater autonomy and independence in the future, we understood that these parents were living in housing situations with their mothers and sometimes their grandmothers, with limited resources and little power in decision-making. This was when I became highly proficient at using the phrase 'doing what is realistically expected' with my staff and parents.

Priscilla, Jean, and I decided we would recruit and hire as many staff as we could with the appropriate credentials; however, we also focused on those with potential, those who were willing to go to school and obtain teaching or early childhood certifications, and others who had the potential and were willing to conduct home visits. It was only then that we were able to make considerable progress hiring staff and turning the tide.

In-Service Training

After reading the performance standards a second time, things were beginning to crystallize. I also read the initial proposal to ensure I was clear about the decisions made regarding our service delivery options, deliverables, and everything it entailed.

Now, my charge, our charge; Jean, Priscilla, and I needed to find a way to convey this knowledge to the staff. We decided that we would only be open 4 days/week, which required parents to have back-up childcare, keeping Fridays sacred for our in-service training. This would provide us with an opportunity to come together at the end of the week, catch up, complete documentation, and come to a mutual understanding of the regulations and how they might inform what we would do with enrolled children and families.

In addition to our approach to service delivery and training\staff to respectfully engage families in their homes, we needed to be clear about our approach to data collection. The data we would collect at intake, the developmental assessments we would use to identify a child who might be developing typically or atypically, which would then inform their individual goal plans, and any other data necessary for reporting to our funders.

This would help the staff address all of their identified needs. We needed to decide how and where we would enter this data and the process we would use to ensure we had a system that would ensure data integrity. I was learning much of this information for the first time while also explaining it to the staff.

There was a training course in Rockville, Maryland, that I attended, which provided me with a deeper understanding of the database system that many Head Start grantees were using to collect their data. The Head Start Family Information System was created specifically for Head Start programs. I had to integrate this new knowledge into my existing schema and then attempt to appropriately convey this knowledge to a diverse group of individuals.

I could not at this time refer to them as professionals because that would be a component of training and a pivotal shift this team would make years later. However, since I am mentioning it now, I will say that having your team shift from viewing themselves as employees to identifying as professionals makes a drastic difference in their attitude, behavior, interactions with families and each other, and their approach to the work.

We were finally moving in the right direction. We had established our intake and enrollment process; we were beginning to write policies and procedures, and service area plans that would guide our work, and we were increasing our understanding of the child and family data we needed to collect. It was beginning to feel good.

Thinking back on this moment, it is rare in the development and implementation process to feel this good so early, because these moments are rare.

Initial Federal Monitoring Visit

"Train up a child in the way he should go; even when
he is old, he will not depart from it."
Proverbs 22:6

We were funded as one of, if I'm not mistaken, six other Wave II Early Head Start Programs in the New York City metropolitan area. There was a great deal of new research about what happens in the brains of babies during the first three years of life. Actor/Director Rob Reiner was an advocate who helped to bring this fact into the national spotlight. His focus on infants and toddlers stemmed from his belief in the critical importance of early childhood development for lifelong success and happiness. This was based upon and highlighted in a 1994 Carnegie Corporation report, "Starting Points." I believe that the timing was right, and the innovators of Head Start used this as an opportunity to expand, funding programs across the country to begin their pre-school services during pregnancy and shortly after birth. This was not only strategic but innovative. These programs were heavily scrutinized. There was confusion about how teachers can educate children so young. The success of this initiative would contribute to Head Start's overall growth. And although Head Start had historically enjoyed bipartisan support, there were naysayers, even within our own ranks, who opposed this expansion. For many people, EHS was akin to a new sibling coming into the family. There were differing opinions on whether this decision would be appropriate. Given that there was so much at stake, we had no other choice but to be successful. Once again, I realized the magnitude of this situation, or so I thought.

The Central Office in Washington, D.C., together with Regional Office leadership and contracted Subject Matter Experts, was responsible for monitoring and overseeing all Head Start Programs. I pride myself now on growing up and having been a part of the Head Start community in Region II. Our office at 26 Federal Plaza is well known for the services offered in the building, particularly for its role in expanding Head Start. Allan Jones and Matt Schottenfeld were the two highest ranking federal staff in Head Start's Regional Office, and they knew their stuff. They had the regulations memorized and could cite them on cue. In my estimation, at the time, Region II had the best leadership; they were politically savvy, and they knew how to support and engage all their stakeholders.

Instead of fearing staff at the regional office, my colleagues and I, who were part of the NYC Cluster of grantees, welcomed relationships with the program and grants specialist and members of the leadership team because they were approachable. If you were fortunate to get them on the telephone and you could articulate a clear question, you would get an answer. I cannot say that it was always the answer you wanted; however, you would receive one. As part of our start-up, Priscilla sent me a copy of a letter she received announcing we would be participating in an initial monitoring visit. Usually calm and composed, Priscilla was excited when we had our face-to-face meeting to discuss preparation for this monitoring visit. I sensed a nervousness that I did not immediately understand. However, I soon realized she was fearful that we could lose the opportunity to provide services to a community that desperately needed them. Her advocacy and concern for this community were surprising yet appreciated. Something in my gut told me she was genuine, too.

After gaining this insight, I immediately aligned with her and committed to doing what was necessary, which would entail galvanizing the team and working longer hours, including throughout the weekend, to ensure we would be ready. I left her office, reflecting on our conversation as I drove back to Far Rockaway. One thing I can honestly say is that I was fortunate to have staff who were as dedicated and committed as I was. It did not take any convincing to get them to latch on to the plan. This would be the first of many occasions when I would be fortunate to observe and interact with the best of humanity. We had two weeks to prepare, and we took advantage of every hour!

I received a call from my assigned Program Specialist, Mrs. Denise Glover. During the conversation, she asked questions to confirm my role, our staffing configuration, and program options. We discussed the schedule for the few days they were to be on site and ended our call. She was pleasant enough, yet something in her voice made me believe that she was formal and thorough. I called Priscilla and provided her with an update after the call. She decided that she would come out on Friday and participate in our weekly staff meeting so we could discuss the monitoring visit with the team. I was happy she was coming out. Having reinforcement was good, and Priscilla had a way of communicating that got our team excited about the work.

Based on conversations with other directors in the NY cluster who had received an initial monitoring visit, there was really nothing to worry about. I learned that they would check for certain things to ensure we had the necessary leadership and governance structures in place. They wanted to ensure there was good fiscal oversight and internal controls, which would ensure we had the ability to be good stewards in how we were managing and using federal funds. They would inquire about our implementation plan, organizational capacity, and any partnerships we developed or were in the process of developing. They also wanted to know if we had enough relevant data on the communities' strengths and needs to inform decision-making. Program governance and our ability to collaborate with parents were another area of focus.

I arrived at the office that Monday morning a little earlier than usual. I wore a dark suit, a white shirt, and a light blue tie. I had a fresh haircut, my shoes were shining, and I was consuming my first cup of coffee when Jean and a couple of the other staff strolled in behind her. I welcomed them and watched as they put away their belongings. They immediately asked if I needed help with anything. I told them I thought that we were good. Now it was about waiting for the monitoring team to arrive. At 8:30 sharp, I saw a couple of vehicles pull up and park in front of our building.

We were temporarily providing services out of the satellite office. I went to the door to greet the monitoring team. A woman named Joyce Carrington led the group; she introduced herself, extended her hand, and gave me a firm handshake. I introduced myself and led them to the conference area where we would be meeting. Joyce informed me that Denise Glover would not be joining the team.

Joyce was the Regional Office Program Specialist that I would be working with from this point on. Tammy Mann, Brenda Jones-Harden & Gambi White-Tenant were the other members of the team.

I stood there in awe, which was evidenced by the look on my face, to the point of staring at them with my mouth open. Four intelligent African American women committed to helping communities provide marginalized families with essential services. Priscilla walked into the office minutes after they arrived, and the entrance meeting began. They were not only knowledgeable but also articulate and extremely supportive. They ran through their list of questions, walked around the facility, and talked with other staff, and by noon, they had a surprisingly good understanding of our philosophical approach to service delivery.

At lunchtime, we were talking as if we were old friends. Joyce pulled me to the side, commended me on our progress to date, and then she began to chastise me, which was really strange. I was told she was a resource and that I should reach out to her for anything I needed. She emphatically stated that I was an African American male bringing much-needed services to the community and that I could not fail. She and the other team members would be at my disposal. This was a happy surprise. I was able to relax a little, take in the moment, and once again reflect on the magnitude of the journey I was embarking upon.

The plan for the afternoon was a conversation with members of our fiscal team, a meeting with members of our Governing Body and Policy Council, a couple of home visits, and a trip to Beach Channel High School to meet our collaborative partners in the Department of Education.

Home Visiting was our primary method of service provision at the time, and we worked hard to select ideal families for the visits. They were two young mothers who were ambitious and bright, and they were beginning to pull things together. In addition, they were advocates for the program.

I was exhausted when the two and a half days were up. I felt like I had gone through an inquisition, a friendly one, might I add; however, they asked us a lot of questions. We did well with our responses. What surprised me was that I not only understood the questions and their rationale, but also answered many of them. They were all related to things we had in place, were in the process of addressing, or would need to address soon. They commended the team for the progress we were making and identified a couple of priority areas we needed to address immediately. However, when they walked away, we knew that we had a great deal of support. We were on our way!

Six months later, almost summer, I was in the conference room, sitting down, talking with a couple of the staff. We were planning an end of the year ceremony with our colleagues at Beach Channel's LYFE Program. Six of our mothers attending high school had successfully completed everything they needed to and were preparing to graduate. I sat with Angela, the social worker, listening intently as she discussed each mother and their plans. A couple were planning to go to college; one was enrolling in a vocational program; one was interested in obtaining a credential so she could work part-time in the program; and the others were going to work immediately. Solid plans for young women who came from histories that did not involve planning. They were already beginning to change their lives. One of the things that stood out to me was that in every situation, the success of these women, their ability to execute their plans, was contingent upon their receiving support from the fathers of their children.

Whether it was financial support, transportation, or support with watching the child they had in common, they were all dependent upon individuals who, up to this point, had not demonstrated they could provide consistent support. Although it was on my radar from the beginning, I had not begun targeting the fathers in any real way. Fast forward a couple of weeks: I am sitting in the conference area eating lunch when Angela walks in and asks if we could meet when I am done. I invited her to sit down, telling her it was okay to talk now as long as she did not have a problem with me finishing my lunch.

She immediately began telling me the plans four of the young women made failed because the men they were counting on for support did not provide it. Hearing this concerned me because it hadn't occurred to me that these fathers might not do what they had promised. The other two mothers had stopped communicating with Angela, and she was worried about them. I was concerned as well; however, I was not surprised.

An interesting thing about life is that unfortunate circumstances can present themselves when we least expect them, which can also lead to unique opportunities. I would not have wished this circumstance on any of these young people, and, of course, we would do whatever we could to help them. However, I immediately began to wrestle with how I could use this situation to our advantage. I sat thinking, and within seconds, the Crisis vs. Opportunity quote flashed through my mind like a neon sign. You see it had been my intention to continue supporting fathers. Taking advantage of the right opportunity was going to be key. I also knew that Andrea, my predecessor, was rare in understanding how important it was to support fathers in a program designed to provide services for young mothers.

My observations of the opinions held by some staff led me to believe that convincing them to engage fathers would not be an easy sell. What is interesting is that I am not sure how I knew this. Reflecting on it now, it must have been based on comments some of them made during our conversations at lunch or during staff development. All of them were good people, dedicated to serving the community, yet their tunnel vision kept them laser-focused on mothers. Recognizing this, I needed to decide how I was going to implement my plan to expand services for fathers. I had to find a way to address and respond to the staff's hesitancy and teach them to engage fathers with confidence.

I remembered from my undergraduate studies how an understanding of research and data helped service providers appreciate the theoretical frameworks used to assist clients, so I needed to find some data to justify why it would be important for us to engage fathers. I could then speak to the notion that if we were seriously interested in helping mothers, we would need to find a way to assist the fathers connected to them. So, I conducted my research, learned a great deal about nothing meaningful, and, however, I felt I had enough to justify beginning to scaffold the staff's knowledge regarding the plan.

As previously noted, the majority of studies concerning fathers have not focused on men from minority groups. Instead, there was a sizeable amount of research on middle-class White fathers and the things that were important to them. The research highlighted the ways they supported their partners, their struggle to balance work and family life, and the time they devoted to engaging their children in developmentally appropriate activities. And while African American and Latino fathers were not part of these studies, at least in my mind, why would they not want the same things for their children and families? This was something I needed to research further, and in doing so, I discovered something quite interesting.

Although I could not find much scientific research, I did find articles and newspaper stories that centered on a negative paradigm. Father's absence, the cost of father absence, the reasons why they were absent, and an inherent belief that they had no intention of providing support for their children and or families. I had heard the saying, "Be careful what you ask for, because you just might get it." This is what I wanted, and yet, what little information I could find suggested my desire to engage fathers would not work with young men of color. A challenge right out the gate, yet something in me was driving me to press on.

The unique circumstances contributing to the young mothers' inability to launch provided a strong justification as to why we need to focus on fathers. So, when I introduced it to the team that Friday morning during staff development, they were open to it. When I began sharing my plan on how important it would be for us to scaffold our knowledge and understanding of how men approach parenthood and why they seemed to struggle, something interesting happened. A number of my staff shared challenges they had observed or encountered in their personal lives, many of which were regrettably negative in nature.

"They weren't men, they were little boys." "All they cared about was making a baby and not taking care of a baby." "They can't take care of themselves, let alone a woman and a child." "My father left my mother with six kids, and we still made it." "Taking care of babies, infants, and toddlers is women's work. Men come into the picture when they get older, when they need discipline and structure."

I listened patiently, understanding and yet a little concerned about the sentiment that men are incapable or not needed. And then it happened. I was not sure it would happen or if it would be an internal or external force; however, a younger staff member shared that she had an amazing father: he was caring and loving to her and her mother, and he was a good provider. She concluded with an emphatic, *I love my father!*" I could not have scripted a better scenario. In that discussion, we had begun to chip away at the complexities of deciding whether to provide similar services to fathers. I believe we all walked away from the discussion recognizing that we needed to do this. The collective work would be figuring out how to do it. I could not understand why; however, a fire was kindling inside me. I had to conceal my excitement and my reservations. Now that I had opened up the proverbial 'can of worms,' I had to deliver.

Significant shifts in the workplace are difficult when there is an established culture and staff have a history of doing things in a particular way. In this instance, our shift, what we agreed to do, was to find a way to provide services to fathers in the same manner as we were servicing mothers. I did not see it as so different, so my goal was to help my staff get on board. By now, I had a staff of about fifteen women, which would grow to twenty-one. Our Home Visiting Program was expanding, and we continued to meet with success, enrolling young mothers, and we were also beginning to identify and recruit fathers. Our strategy was that the home visitors would collect data on the family and be thoughtful and intentional about asking about the child's father.

When the mother was still involved with the father and the relationship was in a good place, it was easy for us to obtain the necessary information to reach out to him. If the relationship was strained, or if there never was a real relationship, just casual sexual encounters, it made it difficult to get what we needed. If he was married or in another relationship, we would likely not immediately obtain any information.

After we received the information, I would conduct the outreach by telephone or accompany the home visitor on a planned home visit. The goal was to have the fathers there so we could meet and talk. This strategy worked well and began to bear fruit because several fathers enrolled after I made contact. I invited them to come to the program for an individual conversation.

We were also beginning to update our marketing and recruiting materials by informing the public that we provided parenting education and other services specifically for fathers. What was interesting was that when the young fathers came to meet with me, I did not see the behaviors written about them. What I noticed almost immediately was concern for their child, coupled with overwhelm and fear. They understood the daunting task that lay before them; they just did not have a clue where to begin. It is important to remember that these were adolescents or young adult fathers.

A large number of them struggled academically and became involved in various systems, such as foster care, group homes, juvenile justice, health care, or the criminal justice system. Society failed these young men by not preparing them for life or the fathering role. Most homes lacked a father figure. No one modeled appropriate parenting behaviors. They wanted to learn because they did not know what to do or how to meet societal expectations. On the other hand, program staff coddle mothers, protecting them and providing them with not only great care but also a wealth of information as they navigate prenatal care, WIC, and other programs geared toward ensuring they deliver a healthy baby.

The comprehensive services Head Start provides are a fitting example of the types of support available to mothers, and yet a young fathers' program, specifically designed to address and respond to fathers' needs, as stated earlier, was a novel idea at the time.

It was time for another staff development focused on our strategies to increase our capacity to serve fathers. We had good examples of young men who were receptive, who participated in home visits, and others who were coming to me for individual and group meetings. It was also going to be important for us to discuss the challenges we experienced attempting to engage and enroll fathers who had not been receptive. We had been scaffolding our knowledge, learning about fathers for about six months.

Today, one of my goals was to explore with the team the notion of starting educational groups for fathers. I was not sure how they would respond; however, to my surprise, the staff embraced the idea. One staff member suggested we enroll more fathers. Others inquired about the appropriate number of group participants, suggesting they needed to be larger for greater impact. I was happy they were on board. We brainstormed ideas and began compiling a list of topics to cover, making sure we included prenatal care and provided additional information on how fathers could support their babies' mothers during pregnancy and after. I left that meeting extremely excited. Good things were beginning to happen!

Three Men and A Baby

"Doing a Small Thing in a Small Place"

Priscilla was really impressed with the work the team and I were doing. She was particularly supportive of our efforts to engage fathers, having learned about the unfortunate outcome for those young mothers. We were having supervision when she shared with me a 'Call for Proposal' to present at a national conference. I'd never presented at a national conference before; however, learning about the needs of young fathers and conducting outreach put me in a position to continually deepen my knowledge and understanding of how to establish meaningful relationships with these young men and to design services that worked for them.

She invited me to review the proposal and mentioned that if I were interested, we could submit it to see if we were successful. I had never heard of a 'Call for Proposals.' Nevertheless, I complied, and a couple of months later, we learned that our submission had, in fact, been selected. What I did not appreciate or fully understand was that only a limited number of programs across the country provided distinct services for fathers. Programs were beginning to recognize it would behoove them to increase their capacity to serve fathers as well.

In January of 1997, I, along with two fathers, went to Washington, D.C., to present our approach to recruiting, enrolling, and delivering services for fathers to other professionals. We were at the Hilton Hotel on Connecticut Avenue. It was a beautiful facility sitting on the corner of a block, in Northwest D.C. Today, it is more popularly known as the hotel where President Ronald Regan was shot and wounded on March 30th, 1981, by John Hinkley Jr., as he was leaving the hotel returning to his limousine after a speaking engagement. It is difficult to fully explain the excitement and anxiety one feels when they recognize the significance of presenting at a National Conference. It is an opportunity to share your experience and unique perspective on how to successfully complete a task with the world. There are several reasons why a particular topic is included in the conference programming.

It might be the only topic addressing a particular approach to this work. Or the climate is such that the field needs to learn more and better understand the issue. Or it might just be curiosity. At any rate, we were presenting two sessions during the Early Head Start National Resource Center's Conference. Our first session would be in the morning on the second day, and the day after, we would present in the afternoon.

I believe the main thing that caught the attention of the conference planners was not just the title, but also our approach and the target population. The session title was Issues Surrounding the Lack of African American Male Participation in Family Support Programs. And our focus was the work we were doing with adolescent fathers. I shared earlier that once I decided to follow what God had placed on my heart and began scaffolding my knowledge in this space to better understand African American males' experience with parenting, I learned how little research had been done on this specific population or, for that matter, the topic.

What I was able to find was an inextricable link between the experiences of enslaved Black men, the challenges they faced maintaining and sustaining a family due to forced separation, and the coping mechanisms they embraced, which, at least to me, explained why they were not connected to their children and families today. Some of it was by design because even when they desired to be present in the lives of their children and families, if the mothers were benefiting from "Means tested programs," the fathers could not reside in the household. These initiatives were created to support families with the greatest financial need, based on set eligibility requirements.

My research took me from Africa, the motherland, to here in America, at one of our seminal historically Black colleges. I am not referring to the renowned Tuskegee Institute, Fort Valley, Bethune-Cookman, or Lincoln University. I am talking about Howard University in Washington, D.C. At one time, HBCUs and Howard University were graduating more African American PhDs than one could imagine, numbers that surpass their current day percentages. Two well-known historians, John Hope Franklin and E. Franklin Frazier, graduated from Howard. J.A. Rogers, a graduate of the Chicago Art Institute and the author of one of my favorite books, From Superman to Man, wrote about history, sociology, psychology, and Theology. He drew upon this rich history to tell a story about Dixon, who was a Pullman Porter, a job that Rogers held from 1909 to 1919. It is a phenomenal story of wit and witticism, a joust, if you will, between Dixon and a racist senator, resulting in a critical change of perspective. The session was going to be provocative but purposeful. I also decided that while I could speak to theory in an intelligent way, I did not feel I could adequately express the sentiment of the young fathers

I was working with, so we built into the session an opportunity for two of the fathers who were actively enrolled in the program to participate and tell their stories.

Priscilla and I were so excited, and as we were planning, I carved out parts of the session I would lead while identifying places where she might contribute. She looked at me warmly, smiled, thanked me, and said, "No, this is your session. I will gladly support you from behind." I would later understand not only her wisdom but the significance of her decision.

At the time, it was easy for me to select a couple of young fathers to accompany me to Washington, D.C. Although several fathers were enrolled in the program, only two fathers were consistently attending groups. Most clinicians believe that having two fathers attending does not make a group. However, I beg to differ. Every so often, a newly enrolled father would stop by and join a group session. I had gotten to know these two fathers really well, a little about their struggles, their passions, their children, and what motivated them to strive to be exceptional dads.

They were now also navigating the responsibilities of men trying to make sense of it all. During rehearsal for this presentation, I was unsure about the outcome and whether it would actually come together. This is again another example of what happens when you trust where God is leading you. There are or will be instances where you have doubts that run deep in your core, and you are inclined to do the total opposite of what your instincts are suggesting you do, and with very little confidence, you proceed anyway, and it ends up working better than you could have ever imagined. I wanted to ensure their comfort in sharing, while also protecting them from any negative consequences.

This would be my first time presenting in such a large venue; we were expecting 75-100 people for our session. Being observant in college, I saw situations where students and sometimes professors attempted to hijack a lecture, which shifted the course of the entire discussion, so I was prepared for a little bit of everything. In retrospect, nothing could have adequately prepared me for the outcome. Although technology was advancing, I purposely chose to capture black and white images of enslaved women, children, families, slave cottages, Black men toiling in the fields, and one extremely popular image of a slave's back being whipped. I turned them into slides and used a slide projector to display these images. This was strategic because I wanted the attendees to reflect on the images as we were speaking. These images, coupled with my calm demeanor as I discussed relevant theories advanced by Howard University intellectuals, and the stories of the two very articulate young men sharing the stage with me, resulted in a well-rounded, impactful presentation.

When we concluded the session, we received a standing ovation. Everyone was clapping. Several attendees were crying, and everyone was displaying heartfelt emotion. I looked across the room and saw familiar faces. Many of the directors who were part of the New York Early Head Start cluster were in the room, sharing in the joy. Priscilla was in the front row, smiling like a proud parent. Tammy, Brenda, and Joyce were in the room, each of them beaming.

My eldest brother, who was in the Air Force at the time and stationed at the Pentagon, was in the front row. I saw not only surprise but also pride in his eyes. This was the side of his younger brother he had never seen. I was happy that he came not only to witness this exciting work I was embarking upon, but also to see his brother in a different light. Finally, a moment and a memory I will cherish for the rest of my life was when Helen Taylor came up to me, grabbed my hand as a proud elder might do, and said, 'Well done, son. Keep up the great work. We need you in Head Start."

I did not know it at the time; however, I would learn later that day that she was the Department of Health and Human Services Associate Commissioner, Howard Alumni, a pioneer, a powerful influence, and a champion for Early Head Start.

My goal in sharing this information in this way and in reflecting on one of the most painful times in American history was not to shame or embarrass anyone. I wanted these directors, leaders of programs across the country, to understand that if they were serious about involving men in their programs, especially Black men, then knowing their history and understanding how it plays out in their daily lives would be an essential first step.

Excerpt: My Talk

"*Good afternoon, my name is David Jones. I am the Program Coordinator as well as the Male Involvement Coordinator for the Visiting Nurse Service In-Step Early Head Start Program, which is in Rockaway Beach, New York. I would like to thank Zero to Three for making it possible for us to be here.*

This is special for me because we are talking about a critical issue, as well as the good feeling I get from the positive response to this workshop. We are here today to share our perspective on the importance of father involvement, cultural diversity, and understanding differences at the individual and programmatic levels, and how this understanding can impact service delivery. I hope the fact that you are here will be to your benefit. I am now even more convinced that helping Head Start and Early Head Start staff recognize the importance of beliefs, value systems, and racism operating within their own lives is crucial for us to understand, in addition to finding ways to work through what we can do about it.

I am going to ask each of you to conduct a self-assessment of the issues we will be addressing today. As an African American male, I can best do this through my experience, yet I hope you will see the correlations that exist across all ethnic groups and communities. African Americans are not the only people who were treated cruelly.

The list goes on and on, from Asia to Europe, the Caribbean, South America, and, of course, here in the United States. There is, I believe, a commonality of suffering when an entire people have been sought out, murdered, tortured, and forced into servitude of various types. For every other group of people, a bond has developed in which the commonality of suffering has drawn them closer. This collective voice has earned these groups respect, opportunities, and an economic voice, opening the door to assimilation.

The difference with African Americans, except for a few movie stars, athletes, religious and or political officials, is that we are viewed as inherently inferior from the onset, before a word is spoken. I was not a slave; my ancestors were, but the question is, why am I often made to feel like one in 1998 America? And while no White people currently own slaves, they still benefit from "white privilege." The experience, the images, thoughts, and perceptions behind slavery are powerful and painfully vivid, and African American families continue to be challenged today. I would like to talk to you about some of those struggles and how they affect our ability to engage African American males respectfully.

From the onset, as part of program implementation, we held a strong belief in the importance of fathers in the lives of their children, and we have struggled for some time with the issue of how to successfully involve fathers. We are beginning to feel as if we are having some success, as two of our fathers are here with me today, and they will be addressing you shortly. We are currently operating our program from the Home-Based model."

Let us talk for a moment about some of the obstacles. E. Franklin Frazier, a noted historian, wrote, 'Because slaveholders often disrespected spousal and parental relationships selling slaves, they created a hostile environment where black two-parent family life never had a chance to take hold, and a strong matriarchal pattern emerged. It has been the Black woman who has held what is left of the Black family together in the form of households where females dominate. The separation of Black families during the enslavement period has had serious implications in terms of the Black man's role as a father and husband.' Racism here in America, the notion of racial superiority, has been akin to a weed growing out of control, stifling the hopes of the Black male's existence. It has choked out the hopes and aspirations of Black men, causing them to seek solace in the evil crutches of escapism, where self-doubt, leaves of absence from the mind, and self-medication have become their refuge. Men who share this or similar experiences are ashamed. Repressed shame can sometimes activate a level of gnawing self-doubt, occasionally reaching the intensity of fully inflamed self-hatred, often present in emotional and antisocial behavior. Many teen fathers are currently struggling to deal with similar aspects of shame, which is so acutely painful that the only thing that suits it is to become invisible.

They escape from this world of norms and conformity and create a world for themselves, gravitating to gangs such as the crips and bloods, where they exist as they choose and make their own rules. Within this new gang community, there is a sense of family, a sense of belonging where members are valued and respected for behavior that is assertive and nonconforming. This behavior usually goes against program standards, which ask for its members to conform and be subservient to a community that has treated Black men with contempt, hatred, and fear.

In many instances, for the first time in their lives, they are happy, begin the reconstruction of an ego broken down over generations, and try to manifest a sense of worthiness. Due to the absence of road maps (a connection to their own fathers), young fathers often don't have a clue about some of the struggles their fathers endured, but they are adamant that their lives will not be the same. So, they fight conformity vehemently, which is how they protect themselves from further embarrassment, hurt, and shame. Suddenly, because they are fathers, family support programs come with their own agenda, attempting to lure fathers back into a world where they are not respected or understood. A world where they never felt connected, asking them to conform when conformity undermines what little self-esteem they have. Practitioners then struggle to understand why fathers are not grateful and do not feel for their child. How can they not feel? Many of the fathers our programs encounter are first and foremost struggling to survive. "A son's experience of his father, whether it is one of absence, neglect, presence, or abuse, is a powerful one, and it directly impacts his sense of himself as a man and as a father." Unfinished business with fathers causes boys to grow into adulthood carrying a 'wounded father' within.

Why is this important, and how does it impact Father/Male involvement in Family Support Programs? The historical context, the effects of slavery, and the breakdown of families have caused a serious lack of trust that resonates throughout the African American experience. It is important to remember that it was within family support programs that minority males were forced to become invisible and deny their contribution to families so that mothers could receive benefits.

Given these factors, combined with inexperience, immaturity, self-doubt, mistrust of the system and its programs, and, finally, an incessant, contagious self-hatred, the task becomes greater as we evaluate our possibilities for the task and intervention.

When a man functions on ego, and society keeps him on his knees, his ego suffers. If one cannot understand how traumatic the breaking down of a man's ego can be and then not providing a sound environment for that man to rebuild his ego, then one would never be able to truly understand or relate to that individual, let alone provide services. Understanding is always better than sympathizing or feeling a sense of obligation. Where does all of this begin today, the awareness of difference and the notion of an inferior status? It comes in many forms, but it is nonetheless dehumanizing. Helping broken men reinvent themselves is not easy. An African American man's ability to fulfill his role as a provider depends upon community systems over which he has little control. The labor force has been known to be a hostile environment for African American men. They suffer from the same employment and economic barriers faced by their fathers, grandfathers, and great-grandfathers. During slavery, Black people had no intrinsic value, and today Black people are still seen as having no intrinsic worth. Money is a measurement of wealth and self-worth. Black men are not thought of as much because they do not have any money; therefore, they are seen as worthless. There is no distinction between the working class, middle class, or professional Blacks. You cannot see what is in someone's bank account. The legacy of slavery still exists today. Ralph Ellison stated, "For Blacks to be accepted in America they must function in a negative fashion. The notion of marginality or living between two cultures helped to fragment the personality."

African American fathers' frustration with the system is often acted out in unhealthy ways, for example, substance use, abuse, and/or

71

violence. We must help fathers see that assertion and aggression are not the way to have others experience them as having worth and to view their power. The challenge for most family-centered programs is finding ways to respond effectively to fathers who seek services.

When exploring more effective ways to get male participation, it is important to understand that if there have not been adequate roadmaps for these fathers to follow, then it is to be expected that they might lose their way. It does not surprise me when people shut down upon hearing the topic of slavery today.

The uneasiness is present because the attitudes held during the enslavement period still exist today. Prejudice still looms; America is still a divided nation. Given what we know about child, adolescent, and human development, those early experiences have a significant impact on one's sense of self. The slave who was struck with the whip endured pain; his dehumanization and shame were felt by all who were remotely connected. Those psychological residuals are ever-present in the men who will walk through your doors. Too often, program designers create services for fathers that do not consider their cultural and historical experiences. We must tailor our intervention efforts so that we are sensitive about these experiences."

If this presentation was not enough to move you, I will add a brief synopsis of the fathers' stories. Albert was left alone in his home to watch over his little brother when he was not more than 7 years old. It is not clear how it happened; however, there was a fire, and Albert was unable to save his younger brother from the apartment.

He struggled with survivor's guilt his entire life. So, in honor of his brother and this loss, he committed to being an actively engaged and involved father, naming his firstborn son, Anthony, in honor of his deceased brother.

Jason met his partner in high school, and they eventually married. His motivation to be a good father was related to his growing up in poverty, seeing his parents struggle with drug addiction, and the loss of his niece. You see, his older brother had a daughter; they lived in the Forty's projects. Again, the story is unclear; however, while his older brother was incarcerated, his daughter was unsupervised for a short time, and she made her way onto the roof of the building and accidentally fell to her death.

Despite these tragedies, both young men were committed to ensuring their children have different outcomes, where they are properly supervised and kept safe. Their stories are real-life examples of the circumstances many fathers have experienced, and this will be part of the history they carry with them. The sharing of these stories, in my estimation, impacted the attendees, which is why there was not a dry eye in the room when we finished.

Chasing Success

"Why can't it be the same for fathers?"

D. Jones

How does one top such an experience? How does one sustain not only the emotional impact but also the focus and commitment? If someone were to ask me how I was able to see to all the work we were accomplishing, I would not have been able to provide a sufficient answer. All I knew was that every day my schedule looked different, and the only day I could predict how my day would go was Friday, because it was my set day for training. Fridays gave me the opportunity to catch up on paperwork, reports, and other outstanding documentation to share with the staff, my boss, the regional office, and community stakeholders. Being busy was good; it kept me alive and forced me to keep my head on a swivel.

Today was my outreach day; I had meetings with other providers in the community. At 10:00 a.m., I had a meeting where community providers came together to strategize how to enhance our collaborative efforts. I was one of the newer members, building relationships and rekindling others I had started to develop when I was here before. I was one of the few men in leadership positions; however, I always felt the women in the community were the true leaders.

They were not only extremely supportive, but they also looked out for me. They understood the magnitude of what I was attempting to do. They wanted me to succeed, and they were determined to help. Ed Williams, a male with power and influence who worked for Assemblyman Gregory Meeks' office, attended these meetings. Sharon Rumley was the Director of the Queens Comprehensive Perinatal Consortium. She and at least ten other Black educators invested in the community and in my success. I always felt a little intimidated when I had to meet with her. She asked tough questions and expected concrete responses. And yet, when I left her office or a meeting where I had an opportunity to dialogue with her, I walked away a little wiser and better prepared to follow through on a particular assignment.

The few men in the room would listen intently during the meetings, and afterwards they would pull me aside, tell me how important the work I was doing was to the community, and let me know if I needed anything to reach out. Despite some of the challenges we were having with the renovations to the space we had selected for our center-based classrooms, things were falling in place.

We were in the middle of an important conversation when my pager went off. I pushed the button to silence it. Two minutes later, it went off again. I once again attempted to silence it, and as I was putting it back on the clip, I noticed that it was one of the staff. She had sent a 911 page. I excused myself from the meeting and found a phone I could use to call the office. It was one of the home visitors, and she wanted me to know that a father was in the office. I said, "OK," and then she said, "What do you want me to do?" Fortunately, this meeting was across the street, and it was only about 10 minutes until the meeting was over. I told her to have him sit down, give him something to read, and let him know I would be there shortly.

I had a habit of shaking my head when I was confused or wrestling with something. I was having a hard time with the fact that this employee did not seem able to translate all of the work we had done around engaging fathers, to welcome him while facilitating a conversation, and to assess why he came into the office. After 6 months of intense training and focus on fathers, this is where we had landed.

When I walked into the office, not more than 15 minutes later, I saw a young man around 19, sitting patiently, flipping through a magazine. He looked nervous and unsure of himself. Mrs. Rumley's office had referred him to our program, and he wanted to know how we might help him. He had a 10-month-old daughter, the courts awarded custody to him, and he was told that we might be able to provide assistance.

I took him to my cubicle, sat him down, and began explaining our program, the services we offered, and how we would work together to help him care for his daughter. I told him that we were increasing our capacity to provide targeted services and support for fathers and that he had come at the perfect time. I provided him with a little more information, completed his intake paperwork, and explained what additional documentation I would need to fully complete his enrollment. I welcomed him and sent him on his way.

That Friday, when I walked into staff development, I had a plan. I really wanted to find a way to reach all the staff and share how essential it would be if we could find a way to serve fathers similarly to how we supported mothers. Once everyone settled in and with Sharon's (the home visitor who reached out to me) permission, I discussed the young father who inquired about our services. I did not talk about what did not go well; I simply asked a question. If a mother walked in the door seeking assistance and support for herself and or her child, how many of you would know how to help her?

Unsurprisingly, all twenty-one hands around the table went up. And then I asked, "Why can't it be the same for fathers?" This was a powerful moment and a significant shift in our understanding of the importance of what we were attempting to accomplish. The discussion that followed, the passion, the insightful questions, and the acknowledgement of their fears, took us to a place we had never gone before.

It, at least in my mind, would go down as one of the best staff development discussions I would have with the core group of staff involved in implementing and designing our services. When we concluded that meeting, every staff member was laser-focused on the discussion and the task at hand: successfully conducting outreach and recruiting fathers. I was fortunate to be a part of and witness this pivotal culture shift.

Community Outreach

It is essential that fathers are present and that they remain vigilant

When you understand the heartbeat and are familiar with the community where you are providing services, there are many opportunities to enhance your approach to the work. When a new organization or business enters the community and begins providing services, it is usually because market research or a data set indicates a need. And as the needs of the community change, providers must also make the necessary adjustments. This enables an organization to stay agile, at the forefront, and primed for enhanced partnerships. When walking or driving through the community, I encouraged my staff, mostly home visitors, to stay vigilant, note changes in the community, go in, inquire about the services these agencies would provide, and ascertain whether they might make good partners. Tell them a little about our Early Head Start Program, our target population, where we are located, and the specific types of services we provide for fathers.

This was strategic because I had been the one to do this before I hired staff. I learned something interesting. Organizations work in silos; they have services that are readily available and are free. All you need to do is sign up for the services.

What was interesting during my outreach to promote the program before we started providing services was that there did not seem to be a genuine desire to help young parents. Of course, I would hear responses like, *'That's really magnificent work, in fact, that's God's work that you are doing. It is a shame for these young people to ruin their lives so early on.'* And there you have it: not only judgment, but quote-unquote professionals who believe they know better than these young parents what they need in their lives. Realistically, they were referring to the huge responsibility these young parents were facing. I could relate to that; however, I understood that young people are not only smart but also resilient. Provide them with guidance, support, and an opportunity, and they will rise to the level not only of your expectations but also of their own.

Everyone makes decisions or finds themselves in situations they reflect on and can accept that they wish they had done something different and/or waited. However, if you provide these parents with consistent support and relevant information, there is no doubt in my mind that they would be able to succeed. I needed not just the home visitors, but all my staff to understand what we were up against.

We needed to be champions for our families because they were not receiving the same type of support from other organizations. Our parents experienced similar judgments in their own families, from people who were supposed to care about them. So yes, there are important things one must consider when conducting community outreach. For me, walking around was like finding hidden treasures. These new discoveries enabled me and my team to re-evaluate current partnerships and explore opportunities for creating others. Operational and service delivery needs shift as one attempts different interventions and then corrects course, so enhancing partnerships is key.

Because of our outreach, we were growing in popularity. The relationships we were building with community partners broadened our reach, leading to an unintended consequence we leveraged to our advantage. By focusing on and enhancing our relationships with these community providers, they became increasingly knowledgeable about our program and would cross-promote and/ or refer when they had a child or family that could benefit from our services. Our numbers were growing, we were beginning to crystallize as staff, and we were locking in not only providing good services for families, but we were also learning and enhancing our capacity to strengthen partnerships. Now that we had our own rhythm, the staff had been trained, they were out recruiting and visiting with families, and I could concentrate on working with our facilities team and the agency lawyers on the renovation of our center-based option.

Initially, I was a fish out of water when it came to renovating a facility and translating all the performance standards requirements that would eventually enable us to provide Head Start services. Square footage, regular cribs, evacuation cribs, it was all making my head spin. The minute you went beyond a final punch list, I was no longer your guy. Priscilla, on the other hand, had more knowledge than me and was patient with me and the process.

Bringing me along and educating me about what should be happening, how I should check in with our facilities expert Jay Margolis, or the general contractor to inquire about when the subcontractors would arrive to do the electrical and plumbing, etc., this placed me in a situation where I was in meetings with her and about five or so high-level officials in VNS, Vice Presidents,

Real Property experts who helped us navigate the bureaucracy and move closer to obtaining our certificate of occupancy. The process took an inordinate amount of time, and when we were only weeks away from obtaining the certificate, we hit a major snag.

I did not know what our next course of action would be, so I called Priscilla and provided her with an update. She made phone calls and then asked me if I could leverage the relationships I built within the community to see if we could get a meeting with the Borough President's office. At the time, the Reverend Dr. Floyd H. Flake was one of our most dynamic and well-respected community leaders. He had been the pastor of the Allen African Methodist Episcopal Church in Jamaica, New York, since 1976. He used his popularity to win the 1986 congressional election. By now, I had developed a good relationship with him because I had been participating in legislative breakfasts with Congressman Flake and other community leaders.

I put out feelers and gathered enough information to better understand how to connect with the Borough President's office to request a meeting. Funny thing is, when God is carving a path for you, there is absolutely nothing that can really get in your way. It took three or four telephone calls before I received a response. This is a good time to mention how important it is to be persistent and not take no for an answer before you can ask your question.

To my surprise, the Borough President, Claire Shulman, wanted to have a conversation with me, so my request for a meeting was timely. She was the first woman to lead Queens as the Borough's President, having served as the deputy to Donald R. Maines, the former Borough President. She changed the way Queens ran its government, ushering the Borough into a new era of growth and economic revitalization, leading the way with the discipline and persistence she learned as a registered nurse during World War II.

I must admit, I got a 'big head' — The Borough President knows who I am and wanted to have a meeting with me.

I could not make the connection between the work she was responsible for and the work we were doing in Far Rockaway, and how they might align. When I called Priscilla to inform her that I was able to schedule a meeting with the Borough President's Office, she was astonished. It was clear to me from her excitement and response that she was just throwing it out there, never really imagining that it would happen.

A little more than a week later, there we were in the Borough President's office waiting to meet with her. She rushed in from another meeting, walked past me, Priscilla, and Laura as if we did not exist, and went into her office. About fifteen minutes later, which was about 20 minutes past our scheduled meeting time, she and her assistant walked out to greet us. Her assistant introduced me as David Jones, Program Director for the Early Head Start Program. She looked at me quizzically, for a moment, and then openly remarked, "Nice to meet you sticking out her hand. I thought this was a meeting with another David Jones." There is no need to discuss what happened with my ego or that big head that was beginning to develop. Because I didn't allow myself to rest in the big-head space for very long, it didn't take much time to deflate. At any rate, she agreed to meet with us because we had taken the trouble to come all the way from Far Rockaway.

It turned out to be a good meeting, albeit short. She did not make any promises, but at least understood our dilemma and said she would investigate. For us, having the opportunity to meet with her and to personally put our situation on her radar was optimal. We never found out what she did, if anything. However, shortly after our brief encounter, the bureaucracy lifted, and we were on our way to obtaining a Certificate of Occupancy.

Sensitivity Training for Community Providers (Enhancing Customer Service)

"A wise son makes a glad father, but a foolish son is a sorrow to his mother."
Proverbs 10:1

When a project or task starts to galvanize, one begins to see things differently. I imagine being so laser-focused on accomplishing a mission or goal gives one a different vision. I can recall that after a successful recruitment or the completion of a memorandum of understanding with a community partner, they would ask, "How did you find out about us, or how did you know our services would align?" Truthfully, I did not really know; I was never sure. However, I was honestly walking on faith. This meant that I would seek out, establish, and build relationships that connect early head start parents with wraparound services to improve and expand the support provided to enrolled children and families. These were instances when my team and I got it right, or when things, as I stated earlier, just seemed to align.

There were other instances where organizations within the community that we needed to align with and build partnerships with to extend or expand services seemed reluctant, or they did not share a similar philosophical approach. Earlier, I referenced the judgmental attitudes our parents experienced from individuals within their family of origin, practitioners, the schools, and organizations that were in the community to assist.

I sometimes witnessed the criticism, the harsh tones, or even worse, the punitive way they communicated with adolescent parents. Executive function is the part of the brain that controls impulse. Adolescent parents, the place where many of them were in their development, given some of the challenges they were attempting to navigate, holding their tongue when they felt disrespected was not a skill they had mastered. So, when they felt judged and or disrespected by an adult, they responded in kind. They would 'clap back' to their detriment because the power dynamic had shifted in favor of the individual operating as a gatekeeper, preventing the parent from obtaining much-needed services.

It was not only me who witnessed this; members of my staff also shared similar experiences when conducting outreach. These were the types of issues we would discuss at our community partner meetings, when many of the leaders of these organizations would come together.

Sometimes they would be aware of what was happening, stating that they were in the process of addressing these issues. If it were current information, it would be hard to accept if this were happening in one of their programs; however, they would vow to take immediate action. One of the members, in their infinite wisdom, explained that the spectacle of older adults judging and talking down to adolescents was not acceptable, and we had a responsibility to help educate these programs about our services, our philosophical approach, and our expectations for what should happen when we referred a client or family to them for services.

What a novel idea! This took me back to my time in Harlem, where I was a community outreach worker providing sensitivity training to organizations on how they could help us support women with their transition back into the community after spending time in rehabilitation for substance abuse. I was traveling around Harlem, speaking at police precincts, during roll call. This was the time when they were receiving briefings at the beginning of their shift.

While it was an opportunity to have a captive audience, you did not have more than fifteen minutes to state your case and explain to them how they could assist you in your endeavor. I remember the first time I did this at a precinct; I was nervous. My experience with the New York City Police Department was not the best, yet I respected the complexity of the job.

As my competence increased, it became more challenging for me to convey the information within the allotted time and elicit a positive response from the group. It always made me feel good when one of them asked a follow-up question, wanted some of my resources, or pulled me aside and said, "Let me know if I can help in any way. I have a brother, a sister, or a cousin who struggles with the same issue."

One afternoon, I was having a conversation with my older brother, James, a New York City police officer working out of the 28th Precinct in Harlem, about my outreach. He was intrigued by what I was doing and shared that he would arrange for me to come to his precinct at some point if I were interested. A month later, there I was at his roll call, talking with his Lieutenant and about twenty of his fellow officers about my work, and how they might be able to support our efforts.

This was a favorable audience; so, the discussion went well over the allotted time. Lieutenant Johnson told me I had a place to come if I ever needed assistance while in the community conducting outreach. I walked out of that meeting with a renewed vigor; I felt safe knowing that these officers, men, and women in blue were looking out for me. So, on Friday, during our staff training, I discussed my experiences conducting outreach in Harlem and how it affected what we were doing. My team and I devised a plan to provide sensitivity training to organizations in the community that needed to enhance their customer service.

--------·～⌣～·--------

Zero to Three (National Conference 1998)

Influencing Others to Walk in the Light

I am not exactly sure when or how it happens; however, pre-presentation jitters tend to subside when one experiences a few successful presentations. The goal then obviously becomes finding a way to sustain that success. It was a year later, and I was back in Washington, D.C., with the same two fathers, preparing to share our success and have them provide updates on their lives, their stories. I am always nervous before my presentations. When I try to make sense of it all, it boils down to my integrity with the content and the audience, and my ability to convey a particular message in a way that says more about what we are doing successfully than anything about me as an individual.

Yes, I am passionate about the topic, and yes, I was trying my best to be obedient in helping others see what I saw to understand the implications of this work. I, of course, would always give credit where credit was due and point out that I knew there were times when God was guiding me and the work because things were transpiring that were well beyond my capability. What these occurrences did for me was keep me humble; at any moment when I might have suggested that there was something truly special about me, I was able to quickly come to my senses and say, no, this is not about you. This is what you are supposed to be doing and where you are supposed to be.

What I can rightfully share is that because of my due diligence, digging into the data that was available, I was learning so much more and increasing my capacity to share this information. I was able to assess the audience when I walked into the room, feed off their energy and nervousness about participating in the discussion, and respectfully engage them in meaningful dialogue. I was educating my team, the Rockaway Community, and now our strategic approach to recruiting and engaging young fathers was informing and influencing programs across the country. We were in our sophomore year, as presenters, which meant we were in a better location, our rooms could accommodate more participants, and we had a favorable schedule. One of our sessions was on the first day of the conference, right after the opening plenary, and the other was the next day in the afternoon.

It felt good to be back in Washington, D.C. The vibe was a little different than it was in New York. What I appreciated about D.C. was that there were so many progressive Black people in good jobs. I interacted with contractors and federal staff during these visits, and I openly shared that one day, when talking to a colleague, I could get used to being a federal employee. While New York is known for its skyscrapers, D.C., at least to me, has massive buildings that cover entire blocks. I always tried to visit at least one museum whenever I made the trip, time permitting. Dinner at Georgia Brown's at least one night was also par for the course. And, whenever possible, exploring the food in Adams Morgan was a special treat. So, arriving the day before my training session began enabled me to enjoy the district, aka "Chocolate City."

The morning of the presentation, I was up early. I went to the gym for a workout, came back, showered, and checked in with Albert and Jason. They were getting ready. I could hear the excitement in their voices.

Things had changed for them. Jason was expecting his third child with his wife, and Albert was actively engaged in a co-parenting relationship. His son's mother, Isabelle, the woman he had talked so lovingly about the last time, was now a formidable adversary. They were not romantically involved and could barely stand to be in the same room together. After two or three couples' sessions, we were able to help them establish a healthy parenting contract. I checked in with him as we were preparing for the session, and on the train ride down to make sure he would be ok, sharing his story. He confirmed that he was good. It was about 45 minutes before our session was to begin, so we decided to grab a coffee and head down to the training room to ensure everything was in order with the audio-visual setup.

We were alone in the room after the audio-visual check. I had the fathers come to a corner of the room where we locked hands and prayed. My prayer was always the same. I asked God to allow us to be a vehicle, I did not want people to see me, but I wanted them to lock in, if you will, anchor into the content, see these two young men who were successfully navigating one of the most difficult jobs a human being could ever do and to give us grace so that we might positively impact a few of the attendees. After that, we would sit quietly reviewing our content, clarifying key points, and wait patiently for attendees to pour into the room.

Waiting to see if anyone will walk through the door at the allotted time can be nerve-wracking. There would always be about five or six people who would arrive early; others would trickle in and sit all the way in the back of the room, and still others would wait until the very last minute just before the doors closed. They would rush in and take their seat if any were available. By now,

I had presented at least fifty times or more, mostly in New York. I had developed a habit of 'working the room,' which meant walking around, singling out individuals, and engaging them in direct dialogue.

I would introduce myself to the early arrivals, ask for their names, a little about their program, and why they decided to attend the session. This would help me understand their expectations, enabling me to address their concerns during the discussion if I had not intended to do so. I was becoming quite skillful in ensuring we were responsive to the attendees and their needs.

The presentation went off without a hitch. We were cooking with gas, sharing relevant content, responding to questions, and engaging the audience in meaningful discussions. People were impressed and inspired. After the session, attendees came to the front of the room. Some people wanted to take pictures with us, some asked if we would autograph their conference programs, and some stood patiently, waiting to ask additional questions. Three or four directors wanted us to come and speak to their program staff. The answers to most of the questions, of course, were based on our availability.

These conversations took place while we collected session evaluations. I really enjoyed reviewing session evaluations, and I reiterated that we take feedback seriously because it enables us to course-correct and enhance the training content. One woman, in her evaluation summary, asked me a tricky question that I was unable to answer without further research. She had to leave, but she shared that a colleague of hers would be attending our next session. The fathers were eating it up. They really loved all the attention and were happy that sharing their stories gave these individuals hope for their programs. We gathered our things and left, heading back to our rooms to change and get out for a little downtime and Caribbean food.

The next day was more of the same. One significant difference was that this time, every seat in the room filled quickly, and we had at least a dozen or so folks standing in the back of the room and along the sides. Hotel staff were bringing chairs in from other rooms to accommodate those who were standing. Word had gotten out about our session.

If I had to compare, this session was even better than the previous one. There was a lot more discussion; we seemed to breeze through the slides, and we were able to just talk with the attendees. I had done my homework, found an answer to that tricky question, and I proceeded to share it with the group. A woman stood up in the back of the room and shared how appreciative she was that we took the time to answer the question. Her colleague asked the question, and she was hoping that I would be able to answer it before the session was over.

Our credibility rose immediately, as evidenced by everyone in the room completing a final evaluation of the session. As expected, the comments and scores were glaring. Mission accomplished, so now it was time to decompress.

A Story in Four Acts

"In the fear of the LORD, one has strong confidence, and his children will have a refuge."

Proverbs 14:26

Writers typically have a vision when they begin to craft a resource that can potentially have an impact on those of us in the helping profession. The interesting thing about a journey such as this is that there are hazards, obstacles, twists, and turns along the way that are unanticipated. Our journey changes us, shifts our perspective, and forces us to not only spend an inordinate amount of time refueling at rest stops, but we also often find ourselves changing direction. The destination or completion of the product looks very different from the author's intent, and yet, if done with honesty, integrity, and a genuine attempt to help others, it hits its mark. Readers are then able to reach their destination, sometimes with a clarity of vision, renewed energy, hope, and enthusiasm.

This resource is based on theory, research, and a great deal of practice examples and real-life experiences of the fathers, families, and staff I have been so fortunate to meet and build relationships with, to give them a lift.

I use the phrase lift with great care because the success of all of the men, women, and children I have been so fortunate to meet was understanding that they were already on the road at varying places and I noticed them, slowed down, stopped, engaged them in meaningful conversation and was willing to either provide them with directions, give them a ride, or help them along the way.

Their success belongs to them, and I am better off because of our interaction and for the experience. With that said, I hope what I've written here is beneficial to you as a reader and, at the same time, helps you help someone along the way as they journey through life.

PART II

HI DAD

A woman shouldn't have to
introduce a father to a child.
To some of us this is strange
bear with me for a while.

I was just a boy of six
or maybe it was five
I'd just begun to run and play
I'd just become alive.

Mamma would call from the window
when I had to come inside
it wasn't so unusual
I cherished this with pride.

Often her call would let me know
dinner was to be served
the ice cream man was up the block
or to get some peach preserve.

Then too were times I dreaded most
her voice was loud and stern upon
entering I knew I'd lost
the extension cord would burn.

I've gotten off my topic
for on this peculiar day
my mother called me back inside
I'd just gone out to play.

As I walked into the house
a man was talking on the phone he
was huge with eyes that burned wearing
too much cologne.

She pulled me close and smiled a lot
I thought that this was strange
this is your father, and this is your son,
Alexander is his name.

It was an awkward moment
but I stuck out my hand
he handed me some money
which made me feel just grand.

He left not to long after
I sat and thought awhile
a woman shouldn't have to
introduce a father to a child!

ENTRANCE

On Ramp

What is more important, the journey or the destination?

An on-ramp, also known as an entrance ramp, is a short road that allows vehicles to enter a highway or other controlled-access road. They are designed to facilitate the safe and efficient transition of traffic from a side road onto a high-speed highway. This is how I have come to think about program implementation. It is initially an intellectual and strategic process, a map, if you will, informing program design and service delivery. I have been designing and implementing services specifically for fathers for years, and, in collaboration with my staff, we developed two nationally recognized fathers' programs. The goal of the program was to assist young fathers by providing opportunities, guidance, and support, enabling them to appropriately position themselves so they can play an active role in their children's lives and development.

What was my motivation? I did not have a healthy relationship with my father because he was not around, which is why this was such a critical issue for me. My senses were keen to the impact of not having a father in a child's life based upon my experiences. Someone once asked why this was so important and if it had anything to do with my father. My response has always been that it is hard to put a finger on what I might have needed, other than guidance, knowledge, and wisdom based on his life experiences. My father gave me life; beyond that, he really did not give me anything I needed.

However, he was an absent yet powerful presence because his absence forced me to be strong. This helped me succeed because the fact that he was not in my life forced me not only to be strong but also to be intentionally different. It also sensitized me to the fact that adult irresponsibility can have a profound impact on children's healthy social and emotional development. His absence and his leaving taught me how to stay and persevere.

For example, I made mistakes early on in my life. The mere fact that he was not there to model for me, to teach me how to navigate the world as a young boy and eventually as a man, and to provide virtues, as previously mentioned, such as guidance and wisdom, placed me at somewhat of a disadvantage. Everything I know today and have used to be successful was a direct result of learning from my failures and from others, because of his lack of involvement. In some respects, my life could have been very different had I known more or if I'd had more paternal support.

Fortunately, God looked out for me, protected me, and provided me with strong Black women who knew how to provide structure and give me enough freedom to grow but not enough for me to hurt myself. When thinking about impact, children who grow up in single-parent families are vulnerable in ways that children who grow up in healthy two-parent families may not be. We learn a great deal about who we are, our identity, by watching our parents. The structure of a two-parent family can offset adverse child experiences, preventing negative outcomes. The key thing in both situations is that children grow up in a healthy environment where individuals responsible for their learning model appropriate communication and interaction, and instill values in them.

Children are resilient, and they can bounce back from a great deal. What they need is love and support so they feel secure in their environment and have someone to go to when and if they face challenging times.

I used to ask myself, "How did I become the one chosen to do this work?" I have come to believe the course my life has taken speaks to an ordained purpose. This was clearly God's doing. Being raised without either of my parents, I could have been angry or bitter, yet I cared enough to not only pay attention to what was happening in my community as it relates to young boys growing up without their fathers. I also found myself doing something about it.

My success, the work my team and I were doing, has been a direct result of decisions I made that were influenced by my belief in God's ability to do what seemed impossible, allowing me to help those tasked with this formidable responsibility.

Adverse Impact

Absent fathers do a disservice to their children, themselves, and society at large. Parenting is the most difficult job we will ever do; however, it can be so fortunate when parents struggle to get it right. One can only deeply appreciate what I'm referencing if they have embarked upon the journey.

At the end of the road, in the golden years, if they abandoned their children or failed miserably due to the lack of a sincere effort, it is my belief that those fathers will be filled with regret. Ego functioning in males can pose as a strength as well as a weakness. As a means of strength, males tend to exhibit egos that encourage, excite, and sometimes hyperbolize their self-esteem, which in turn gives them a greater sense of pride in achieving or performing. This is a strong quality that can push a male to strive further or work harder. However, the opposite side of this conundrum is that an inflated ego can be a limitation if it leads to a false sense of self or reality.

In addition, when fathers are not present, it creates a longing for male guidance, which is why these young men gravitate to gangs. It provides a sense of family, protection, and financial support. Without positive male influence, young boys, who will eventually become fathers, do not see other alternatives. On at least ten occasions, during interviews with reporters about my work with young fathers, my response was always the same.

"After more than 25 years of doing this, I am still stunned by the question frequently asked of me, which is, "Why is this work important?" It is a common question because people want to know or strongly believe they are speaking for the greater population when they ask why, and is it making a difference? Can I measure impact? One only has to be a fly on the wall or an active participant in a group session to witness the level of sophistication, complexity, and the freedom with which the fathers speak. Yes, the work is extremely important, we are making a difference, and we are beginning to measure impact."

Witnessing how determined fathers are to care for and provide for their children, something in life better than what they received, is inspiring. It is important to share that Fathers First and The Bronx Fatherhood Programs were unique in that they were derived from a model that I created. My experiences, conceptualizing and bringing to life the 'Fathers First Program' enabled me to make a pivotal shift when we advanced to a full-service operation for fathers in the South Bronx. Fathers First entailed taking the best components of respectful service provision and applying them to young fathers, with an emphasis on communication, education, and vocational training. It was here that we learned there is a process they go through as they transition and accept services from providers.

Even if or when the staff are respectful, fathers go from non-committal to curious, to initially engaged, to minor commitment, to involved, and finally to fully engaged. Recognizing these factors helped when we transitioned to the Bronx.

The Bronx Fatherhood program was father-driven and individualized based on their expressed needs. Yes, as experienced practitioners, we provided the structural components built around management and oversight systems that enabled us to track and measure the fathers' progress; however, when it came to making decisions regarding their goals, we deferred to them or, at a minimum, helped them ground their goals in reality. My work with young men and fathers provided insight into their needs and revealed that many programs often overlook key factors when designing services for fathers, particularly for young fathers. My clinical expertise and skills were another essential component of our model.

Research suggests there are hundreds of benefits to having fathers involved in their children's lives i.e., separations, transitions, accelerated heart rate, fragile infants in the neo-natal intensive care unit, educational, emotional stability, security, attachment & bonding, just to name a few.

It is important to note that our model also supported mothers. We focused on the day-to-day physical care of the children, nurturing, bonding, educational support, and the co-parenting relationship. One of the things I am most proud of is helping to bring the importance of father involvement/engagement into the national forefront, especially with respect to African American and Latino males. There were articles and research suggesting that these two groups, especially adolescent fathers, were not actively involved in their children's care and were not interested in doing so, which was clearly not the case.

As previously mentioned, our presentations across the country garnered widespread attention as we challenged belief systems and myths. What has been especially rewarding is the relationships I have been able to build with these young men in the process of assisting them in healing and making decisions to change their lives.

Act I: The Engagement Phase (Fathers First): Emphasizes the notion of operating on faith, while living in a place of uncertainty, and at the same time elevates fathers' capacity to comfort and demonstrate abilities and capabilities that refute the notion that they are inept as caregivers.

Act II: Bringing It Home (The Bronx Fatherhood Program): It is emblematic of the growth and lessons learned by listening, being patient, and trusting the process. A process that enables others to see the ways in which fathers can inspire their children and families.

Act III: Fathering Me: The Long Walk Home: It is about redemption, explaining how a dedicated professional's decision to walk away at the height of a phenomenal experience allowed him time to take a much-needed pause, to evaluate his perspective and to reflect, after missing the work terribly, finally deciding to share experiences that he believed would be beneficial to the field. What is important here is that fathers not only have the innate capacity to teach their children, but if we are willing, they teach practitioners as well.

Act IV: Making the Case (As a Coach, Consultant, and Trainer): It brings us to the current day. Now a seasoned practitioner, galvanizing a host of experiences, I'm seeking ways to give back and share pivotal lessons learned, anchoring in the fact that it is fathers' love that permeates all their efforts to care for, nurture, and provide for children and families as they navigate their own personal journey through life. Join me as I embark upon this new journey.

An Evidence-Based Model of Father Engagement

There are no shortcuts to any place worth going.

I arrived at the Visiting Nurse Service of New York with a passion and a commitment to engaging fathers, enhancing and supporting them, and the role that they could play in their children's lives. As I reflect upon it now, I am certain the seeds were planted in the blood of my ancestors. Their strength runs through my veins, and it is because of them that I dare to be bold enough to believe that I can make a difference. My mentors were family members and educators who saw things in me that I could not see in myself. The educators I am referring to were descendants of slaves who, under the threat of death, found a way to educate themselves so that they could educate others. Not only did they have the fortitude to educate themselves, but they also reached back and taught us.

When I attended Cousins' Elementary in Sardis, GA, I had the great fortune to sit with at least three of the same Black educators who taught my parents. It is funny to think about it now, and it was painful as I reflect; however, when our schools were segregated, despite having limited resources, we fared better because the teachers cared. They not only invested in the children's ability to learn, but they also staked their reputation on it. That is why anyone who was fortunate to have that experience understands the value of a good education, where the teacher invests in your success.

My evolution into this work is vibrant, yet it is not complete, as each day, observing children, men, and women and interacting with them in developmentally appropriate ways, I make new discoveries, ushering me into a deeper understanding of who I have become amid supporting families.

How did I get here? I was a stowaway in the veins of my ancestors who arrived on slave ships, individuals who endured much so I would be free to be me. Freedom in America is relative, and yet embracing one's sense of individuality and uniqueness can come with a price. However, in the children and families, I see my story, a story filled with hope.

In 1994, I worked at St. Luke's Roosevelt Hospital. With my Bachelor of Psychology degree in hand, I began working as an Outreach Worker/Research Assistant in the Second Chance Program, a drug treatment program serving women. All the women had used drugs during their pregnancies, giving birth to babies addicted to cocaine. Being a young father at the time, I was not in any position to judge; however, I struggled daily with questions about how and why. How could they? Why would they? Shameful to admit it, I knew the answers.

Living in the wealthiest industrialized nation, among all the civilized nations, we still have not found a way to prosper without preying upon individuals at the lower level of the American Caste system. I empathized and sympathized with babies who cried incessantly, longing for their mother's touch, a motherly touch, or anyone's consistent touch to help them self-regulate. Within this program, I quickly learned to thank God and appreciate that I was supporting the development of my own children as they met their milestones.

The Second Chance program provided a full array of services for enrolled mothers, which included daily drug testing, individual counseling, medical assistance, and narcotics & alcohol anonymous groups. My role was to conduct outreach to newly enrolled mothers, escort them to entitlement appointments, and conduct joint home visits with the social work staff. Although it was not required, I took every opportunity I could to visit the child development center to help Tessa, our certified child development specialist, care for the children.

The childcare center provided much-needed nurturing and physical care for infants who were sometimes incapable of self-soothing. There were others who would eventually regulate; however, this only happened after prolonged periods of holding, caressing, and stroking. The children cried incessantly, and yet, I rarely witnessed Tessa's frustration. She welcomed my assistance and quickly reminded me to cover my shoes with the "blue booties" before entering the classroom. I always liked interacting with and spending time with the babies.

I had a younger brother and a dozen cousins when I was growing up. Even though I was not much older, I felt a responsibility to look out for them. As a young adult, now with children of my own, I find comfort in spending time with young people. There is genuineness and purity in their innocence, and they exude optimism.

While working in the program, I learned to appreciate the comprehensive care that Second Chance provided these women.

I cannot honestly say I agreed with the program or its services. I was hopeful, so I did my job to the best of my ability. There were instances where, if they were compliant, listened to their counselor, and were able to stop using drugs, they would get a second chance at life. Then they would attempt to comply with the Department of Children and Family Services' requirements to have their children returned to them.

Unfortunately, this was a rare occasion since these women struggled constantly with sobriety, so much so that I frequently found myself in case conference meetings, listening and yet not fully engaged. In fact, there were times when I hate to admit it, I sat not paying attention, bored out of my mind because there did not seem to be a genuine interest in helping these women change their behavior. I recognize this is not a popular stance, and it is more of an indictment of our social service system; however, I could not discern whether the intention was to help them or keep them dependent on the program. My experience in the social service field resulted in my developing insight into what I call an essential component of the American dilemma. The decision to focus on intervention as opposed to prevention. Intervention perpetuates the problem, and rarely, if ever, contributes to meaningful solutions. Intervention is more costly and time-consuming than prevention efforts, which are geared toward providing awareness and education before a particular service is needed. Selfishly, it keeps us in business, and on the other hand, it destroys lives.

While I had no specific role in deciding the outcome of the cases, nor was I ever asked my opinion, I could not understand why there were so many excuses made for women who continued to not only manipulate the system, but also constantly placed their children in harm's way. One excuse after another led to yet another intervention suggestion. What became clear after sitting in about ten of these meetings, when it came to permanency planning, the staff never mentioned the fathers connected to the women and children.

All of the children were enrolled in kinship foster care with other family members, most often maternal grandmothers, aunts, cousins, family friends, or distant relatives, who were strangers to the children.

I cannot remember one occasion where staff considered the biological father as a realistic option. Wanting to make sure I was not being overly sensitive as a young father, I checked in with Maurice, the only other male on the team. He was a father of two young sons and an outreach worker as well. I wanted to ensure this was not just my observation or personal bias.

Having worked in the program much longer and understanding the nuances of these decisions better than I, he enlightened my thinking by stating the obvious: the program's culture was not only female but also anti-male. I was taken aback by his comment. Could that possibly be the case? I was not certain; however, it made sense.

That afternoon, I found myself on the #2 train heading home to Brooklyn, wrestling with this fact. As an actively engaged father, I could not wait to get home to interact with my children. To hear about their day and just observe their growth and development. Painfully reminded of my own experience of growing up without my father, I took my role seriously, far too seriously, vowing I would never separate myself from my children nor would I minimize the significance of my role as an educator, nurturer, guardian, and provider.

I was not surprised when I found myself sitting in my supervisor's office, struggling to ask whether there was something we could do about the way the case conferences were structured. I was surprised at how little time it had taken me to make up my mind to discuss it with her after my conversation with Maurice, given that I can be quite pensive at times. When she wanted further clarification, I asked why none of the staff advocated for the biological father as a viable option in these permanency planning decisions.

Elizabeth Carr was one of the reasons I entered the Social Work profession, a fact she is not aware of; however, if she were, I am confident it would make her smile. She was an African American sister who held firm to what little culture we as African Americans were able to preserve.

Frequently, dressed in traditional African garb, I witnessed how she interacted with colleagues. She was not only intelligent but also savvy, with a knack for calling out injustices. She was incisive, decisive, and emphatic in her responses, and she would let you know she valued your failed attempt at the joust. During conversations, she would pounce on bias or discriminatory comments with fervor. It was interesting to watch.

She clung to the National Association of Social Work Code of Ethics, referring to and quoting from it so much that she aroused my suspicions about her co-authorship of the document. I enjoyed my supervision sessions with her. I usually left inspired and motivated to be intentionally different in how I not only understood but also approached the work. I felt the trust we had developed afforded me the opportunity to be honest with her.

Her response to my inquiry not only shocked and surprised me, but also disappointed me. "How is it that these permanency planning decisions are constantly being made, and there is no consideration of the father?" Liz, as most of us called her, spoke comfortably not only for herself but for many of the other women in the program who believed it was the men involved in these women's lives who were responsible for their substance use; therefore, they were not in any better position to care for the children than the mothers. I was stunned!

It had been a long time since so many thoughts and questions raced through my mind simultaneously that I was unable to respond or articulate a question, reminiscent of my stuttering days as a child.

Years later, I witnessed, at a research conference, the constant barrage of questions about evidence. Individuals who are presenting content at conferences or professional development training must not make faulty generalizations without backing up their statements with some form of data.

Similarly, I, too, wanted, no, I needed proof that such a scathing accusation had merit. Sensing my struggle, she suggested I develop a plan to do something about it and get back to her. I was deflated and disappointed. I questioned whether the conversation we just had was even worth it. Walking down the hall to the office I shared with Maurice and Michelle, I relented.

I could not tell at that moment whether I was successful in getting Elizabeth to understand and appreciate my concerns. If I had, it would have been a pyrrhic victory at best. So, I am guessing it does not surprise you to learn that I began conducting my own research.

No matter what I read or where I searched, I could not find anything to substantiate Liz's comments about men introducing drugs to their partners. As previously shared, research about fathers focused on White middle-class males, and the struggles and triumphs they experienced as fathers embracing increased expectations of the father's role.

The substance abuse literature addressed addiction, relapse, and eventually treatment options. This led me to decide I would engage fathers, yet I had no clue how to do it. To be honest, I started my initial fathers' group to prove her wrong. I wanted to see if I could help young men break a negative perception centered around Black fathers' absence. I also, reflecting on my mother's experiences, wanted to help mothers who were struggling, and I wanted to change negative outcomes for children.

So, when I began outreach to some of the fathers connected to the women enrolled in the Second Chance Program, I was surprised by their immediate engagement and willingness to talk to me.

As unbelievable as it sounds, when I inquired why a couple of them never came to the program or shared their concerns about their children's well-being, one father told me no one ever asked or invited him to participate. No one asked for their input! This was astonishing and exciting to me at the same time because it provided me with just what I needed to demonstrate that these men were not only capable of caring for and providing for their children if they were the beneficiaries of the same support that moms received, but also willing.

Five basic principles I used as a frame for fathers' support groups:

- It is not easy to define a father's role,

- It is a father's responsibility to invest in their children,

- Investing in a child's education and providing guidance, support, and structure is an essential part of a father's role,

- Fathers, teach your child everything you know

because it lays a foundation and helps prepare them for their future,

- The time you have with your children is priceless, because it passes so quickly, so use it wisely.

Facilitating Fathers Support Groups

An 18-month-old infant begins crying at 2:17 a.m., awaking her parents. On cue, her 19-year-old father rises, gently touching his partner, the baby's mother, on the shoulder. He mumbles with a half yawn, "I got this one," as he goes to his only child. In his mind as he approaches the baby's crib, he is already wondering if the cries are because the baby is hungry or are they because she is wet? He is not sure, but he is prepared to manage whichever situation awaits him. Later that week, during the father's support group, he updates other fathers about his week since his last group. He shared what is new in his child's development, what is going on at school, and how well his communication is going in his relationship with his partner. His highlight is surprising and causes a stir as he excitedly talks about his sense of accomplishment and competence at being able to not only address but also identify his daughter's particular need.

I really learned the importance of group process when collaborating with fathers by just digging in and starting the group. In most cases, when I have been the facilitator, the participants have a common historical experience that brings them to the group (all parents or soon-to-be parents), or they believe they can benefit from the group by sharing their experiences and learning from others. The goal of the group is to help fathers understand the process, their roles as parents and partners in their respective relationships, and to further appreciate their children's developmental milestones, and the benefits of learning to communicate more effectively. The group sets the parameters, including rules like confidentiality, respect for others, and the option to not share or to disclose only what one is comfortable sharing. There are set days during the week when the group meets, and food is provided.

The initial phase of the group is to help fathers become comfortable with the process and with each other. The notion of coming prepared to discuss, ask questions, or participate in some meaningful way is also important. At the beginning of the group, father's check-in and after that they spend at least 5 to 10 seconds in front of the mirror. The mirror represents their conscience. It provides them with an opportunity to quietly reflect, assess, and evaluate their functioning over the past week. We all know the mirror does not lie; it will always tell the truth.

If a father can stand in front of the mirror and be pleased with his image, then, in most instances, he is living a life of good decision-making. My team and I are usually observing the process to see if any of the fathers react differently during this process. If we notice anything, we give them time to share, or we might probe a little to help them disclose.

I model for the fathers by opening the discussion and sharing something about my week since we were together last. It is usually something about my co-parenting relationship or something that has occurred in my child's development that I was either delighted by or frustrated by. I share how I managed the situation and why I chose to respond in that manner. If there was a pivotal lesson I learned about me, my partner, or my child, I would share that as well. When I plan the group session, I identify points of emphasis or take-home messages for the fathers that I try to interject throughout the discussion.

On most occasions, however, the discussion is free-flowing. I am also keenly aware that not all facilitators will necessarily be parents; however, a process like this is useful in helping fathers relax and begin to comfortably share their own experiences. In the second phase, we address their understanding of the parenting role, whether in a relationship or not, and any challenges to fulfilling that role. This is a time filled with amusement and laughter as participants begin to better understand how culture and our family of origin influence our parenting beliefs, whether we have ever had the opportunity to practice them or not.

We discuss common misconceptions about parenting, clarify and correct misinformation, and, if not readily available, provide resources during subsequent groups. This helps the facilitator or individual responsible for running the group compile a list of items to discuss, further emphasizing the collaborative component of the group process, as these future topics are based on comments and inquiries made by fathers during group sessions.

The third phase is discovering ways fathers can carve out the time to create opportunities to be actively involved with their children, and then having them share with the group the joys and challenges of doing so. This is a key area of focus and underscores the significance of societal-prescribed roles.

Fathers experience undue pressure attempting to fulfill their roles because they feel they are not responding as expected unless they fulfil the societal-prescribed definition of a financial provider.

This dilemma frequently prevents them from being involved in a meaningful way. While it is important for them to consider the financial aspect of their role, in my mind, that is only one part of their role as it relates to their children. I help them expand on this definition by bringing in information on the importance of attachment, bonding, quality time with children, and social and emotional connection. We address developmentally appropriate activities and their role as educators. When fathers feel more competent, they bring their children to the group. Seizing the moment, I attempt to further illustrate developmentally appropriate interactions as they communicate and respond to their child's needs.

The group process is a time to educate fathers about many of the unpleasant realities of the world, how to contend with their sense of self, and why they may not feel so good about their options. We talk about racism and discrimination, and how ever-present these factors are in their lives, and how they influence decision-making. We discuss how to successfully navigate the system from within, legally, rather than creating their own rules, which increases their chances of success.

The final phase of the group is looking specifically at personal goals. I discuss the importance of being consistent and persistent, not only in deciding what they would like to do, but also in staying true even when facing adversity.

We explore the difference between setting goals and actively working towards them, juxtaposed with dreaming, as in the case of the lottery. They walk away with plans that, if properly executed, will place them in positions where they are satisfied with their employment situation, actively spend time with their children, and improve their co-parenting relationship.

One of the most important things I have learned about group process is that traditional methods sometimes do not work. I created an equal playing field, so to speak, where at any given moment, a participant, someone other than the identified facilitator, can quickly and effortlessly step into that role. So, not more than a month after conducting my initial outreach to the fathers, I requested permission from Liz to start my own fathers' group.

We began with about 3 fathers, and eventually the group grew to about 6 or 8 fathers attending regularly. Initially, they were just rap sessions, getting to know them, a little about their past, and their goals for themselves and their children/families. I would introduce a concept about fathers to assess their level of understanding and whether my assumptions were correct. Eventually, the fathers' groups became more structured around a particular theme that challenged their belief systems.

One group in particular still lives in the front of my mind. The theme for that particular group was about seasons of change. A subliminal goal of all the groups was to introduce new knowledge, have the fathers grasp the concepts, and incorporate the information into their current way of thinking.

I hoped that taking in information this way would contribute to growth and development over time, leading to lasting change for fathers, their children, their partners, and their community. I asked the fathers about their capacity and approach to completing a puzzle at ages 2, 5, 7, and 20. After a rich discussion in which the fathers shared varying yet similar opinions, we agreed that putting a puzzle together is a cognitive function. For a toddler, it can become a marker of success, where they learn to demonstrate patience, persistence, and tenacity, where at twenty, that toddler is now able to put together a 1,200 or 2,500-piece puzzle, a more complex cognitive function with ease.

This, of course, is the cumulative effect of learning over time. As I scanned the room, it became apparent to me that most, if not all, the men in the room understood. They were able to make the connection between being consistent in their children's lives and how commitment provided them with an opportunity to contribute to their children's ongoing growth and development. One immediate impact they identified was the importance of learning self-regulation. Instead of arguing with their child's mother, something all of them had done in the past, they tried to strike a balance and find a way to have a healthy discussion.

Now that they are aware that their children are watching, and they understand the impact arguing can have on their child's sense of security, they attempt to avoid arguing in front of their children. Arguments reflect one's desire to win or not lose, while a healthy debate frames the discussion in a positive way and leaves one open to compromise if a logical solution is offered.

Healthy discussions or debates are a natural outcome of positive communication. This ability to analyze and assess situations and to strive for positive outcomes during difficult communications is a skill that will serve fathers well in their relationships with their children and partners, and throughout life.

A wise father, after having lived through trials, said during the group meeting, "In all my life, I've never been in a healthy relationship." In that moment, I had to think hard about that statement because, except on rare occasions, we all learn how to be in healthy relationships from failed relationships. This is relevant because we are in the business of educating and caring for children. To do that effectively, we need to be impartial and support parents in their ability to enhance their children's development. Fathers and mothers each play a significant role in shaping their children's understanding of what it means to be in this world. Our children do not grow up in a vacuum.

I am frequently reminded of the commercial where a father walks into a room and catches his teenage son smoking marijuana, so he screams at him, "Where did you learn to do this?" The kid defiantly looks up and says, "I learned it from you!"

The family of origin, in most cases, is the initial training ground where young people learn about life, love, commitment, and how to co-exist within the family. This is where they establish relationships with family members and observe the relationships they see around them. These experiences become a permanent imprint upon our brains. Unfortunately, for an increasing number of young people, social and economic challenges have undermined the family structure, and families living in poverty often experience relationships filled with chaos and confusion, void of commitment, love, and support because of the daily stressors of life.

Our charge has been, and will continue to be, to level the playing field and help parents in their efforts to provide a playground experience for children. In my observation of children on the playground, they are not only playing; they are learning. However, what is most important about the playground is that it is where they are most free. They feel safe, filled with innocence and hope. We could use more of that in the world.

Victor's Story

Victor never knew his dad, at least not in any real sense of the word. The only memory he had of his father was his infrequent visits to the Bronx when he was seven or eight. His father would walk him to the store, and they would return to sit on the stoop and eat oatmeal cookies. Just when Victor begins to get comfortable and start feeling secure sitting in his father's shadow, his dad disappears again. He shared an unpleasant event that occurred 7 years later. When Victor began presenting challenges for his mother at home and at school, she reached out to his father. Not long after, he arrived on the spot as the disciplinarian. He beat Victor until he lost consciousness. Afterwards, his mother threw his father out and never allowed him back in the house.

That was the last time he remembered seeing his father alive. A couple of individual sessions and fathers' support group meetings later, Victor candidly discussed some of the ways in which he had grown into adulthood.

"My daughter is the light of my life. I am scared because everything associated with being a father is hard. My girl and I used to fight; now, we just argue. At first, we argued all the time because I thought just being there and not running away from the responsibility, like my father and so many other men used to do, was enough. Then I had to learn to do so much more. I had a good understanding of what I missed not having my dad. The groups really helped me with that part, which was not easy to deal with, and I remember getting angry.

For a long time, I was not sure why. One day, I called my father to curse him out, but I did not have the nerve to go through with it, so I hung up. I still feel like I will call him one day. Anyway, I had to learn to help with everything, feeding, bathing, and looking out for her when she is sick. I don't get any rest, but it keeps the arguing down, and my girl and I are getting better. I really like it when my daughter and I are alone, and she falls asleep on my chest. She likes the heartbeat, and I like her warmth!"

Establishing trusting relationships is essential in all work with fathers. The clinical experience needed to engage a father with a similar history to Victor's in individual sessions is not something all programs can offer. While Victor came to the center willingly and began participating in groups, aspects of his perception of his role as a father needed refinement.

He had a grandiose, idealized view of what his father had and had not done for him. Victor was not clear about his role as a father. His attendance was poor at first; however, as I began to explore his history with him further, it became clear that he did not have any real connection with his father. His only connection was with his mother, a relationship filled with disrespectful communication, inappropriate expectations, and an unhealthy interdependence between them.

In addition, Victor held a great deal of resentment and displaced anger towards his mother, which stemmed more from his father, whom he idolized. It was too difficult for him to come to grips with that reality.

He admittedly took on the parentified child role to help support his mother with the demands of single parenthood. At the same time, he denied himself the childhood he deserved. I questioned how one so young could be so mature and so ready to embrace the fathering experience, and it became clear to me that he had been fathering himself all the while.

It took time before he was willing to embrace this notion. A half-dozen individual sessions and groups helped move him along the way. After being involved in the group for a little over a year, Victor discussed his relationship with his mother. He described it as being exemplary, one in which they spent quality time together weekly and where they could communicate about anything. I watched as he spoke. Other group members appeared almost envious of his relationship. Had I not been aware of how unrealistic his portrayal was, I would have been envious.

The real story was that, as a child, he had hardly ever lived with his mother. When he became too much trouble, he went to live with his grandmother. He attempted to return to live with his mother; however, this only lasted a short while, as she struggled to manage her own life. They lived in three different homeless shelters until he was sent to the group home, where he lived until he graduated from high school.

Victor still visits his mother periodically on weekends, bringing gifts and food items she asks him to bring. She currently lives in a rooming house. She still could not bring him home today, even if she wanted to. It is also important to mention that his displaced anger towards his mother carried over into his relationship with his child's mother, and the abuse he experienced as a child and witnessed within his home (his mother was in an abusive relationship) influenced his understanding of what he thought was acceptable in a relationship.

When I returned to the Visiting Nurse Service, I had about six months' experience running support groups for young fathers. I took from my own personal experience as a father, my experience of not interacting with my biological father, and finally, my experience of having my male perception shaped and influenced by community elders, uncles, and strong Black women. I had gained considerable experience initiating, developing, and running the support group at the Second Chance program. I learned what I still believe to be my most valuable experience: providing individual psychotherapy to adolescents when I worked at Hamilton Madison Settlement House and in three different elementary schools on the Lower East Side of Manhattan.

The Head Start program's focus was targeting adolescent parents as well as enrolled infants and toddlers. I drew from insights gained from participating in family meetings, group facilitation, my experience as an emerging therapist, and my parenting role to guide my understanding of what we were attempting to do. There were parallels I could rely upon to help me understand my role in supporting children and families. I made the decision early on that, as a program, we would serve families, not just mothers and babies. This meant, at a foundational level, that as we were developing policies, procedures, and protocols for the design of the program, we would be thoughtful about considering ways of involving fathers. In June of 1997, we began offering fathers support groups.

What was clear to me was that I was not part of the initial planning for the development of the Early Head Start programs. I had to buy into someone else's vision. For this reason, one of the essential tenets of launching an effective program, in general, not necessarily father-specific, is to ensure that everyone who comes on board understands the vision and the mission of the program. What specifically is it that you are attempting to accomplish, how, and why? It is also important for the individual leading the programs' implementation to be fluid, understanding the need to finesse and/

or tweak the vision in ways that support and encourage continued growth, based on feedback from staff and other stakeholders as appropriate.

From Theory to Practice: An Evidence-Based Model of Father Engagement

The greatest oak was once a little nut who held its ground.

I was very happy working on the lower east side, providing individual psychotherapy to adolescents. I did not have a real desire to leave. As previously mentioned, a former colleague called and asked me to consider applying for the position to direct the implementation of the Early Head Start program, yet I was reluctant. I agreed to consider the offer, and my investigation of the organization led me to believe, based on its history, that it would provide me with something my current agency could not: advancement in the form of real opportunities for continued personal and professional growth.

Do not get me wrong: the skills I learned providing individual psychotherapy without a clinical degree have given me a lifetime of understanding and skills that continue to serve me well today. However, if I were to improve, I would need an advanced degree and additional training. After months on the job, it was clear that the administrator for the Maternal Child Health Division, my supervisor, was very supportive of my desire to design services for fathers. It became immediately apparent to me that another essential component of successful program development entails a rich environment for innovation and supervisory support. When I reflect on the Fathers First program and attempt to answer the question of why it has been so successful, I would have to go back to the performance standards. The guidelines enhanced my understanding of wrap-around services. It emphasized an integrated approach to serving children and families, which I applied to my work with fathers. Add to that a firm belief that men can appreciate and are willing to participate in programs that provide responsive, timely services designed to specifically address their needs, and you have a formula for success. Given that there was no framework or blueprint for building a successful father's program, this inherent belief in their capacity and commitment to success was essential.

A willingness to constantly modify the program design was a key factor, combined with an understanding of male ego functioning. I also came into the situation with a hypothesis. I grew up without a father present in the home, a reality in many underserved communities; however, it is grossly overrepresented in underserved, marginalized communities. One of the greatest misfortunes was the scarcity of positive male role models. Despite this fact, I was able to observe that these men, although not always functioning appropriately in relation to their families, were interested in being involved. They were present, and if not consistent, they had a connection to their children, if not to the entire family.

The way the media portrayed African American and Latino fathers, for the most part, was irresponsible at best. They wanted to be involved with their children and provide for their families.

My hypothesis was that if they

had solid support and received education about how a father's absence further compromised their families' situation and adversely impacted their children's opportunities for success, this would provide the motivation they needed to begin learning how to do something different.

This new information might motivate them to take advantage of support systems that were becoming more available in the mid to late 90s, given the influx of women in the workforce, and the advancement of stay-at-home dads, which also increased the number of men involved in caregiving activities, resulting in fathers expanding their definition of what it means to be a father.

Fortunately, the environment was ripe for programs that were willing to invest in male/father involvement initiatives. In my estimation, too often, men subscribed to the financial provider role, even when it was painfully clear that the playing field was not level with respect to their equal opportunities to provide for their families. At one point, unemployment for African American males in New York City was as high as 51%.

My understanding of how to support fathers developed a couple of years into the program, when I found a curriculum, the Partnership for Fragile Families – Young Fathers Curriculum. It was comparable to many of the things I had begun to learn about the challenges and obstacles men face in developing into competent parents. It soon became clear that their development as men was a major area of focus, as the two developmental trajectories, fatherhood and manhood, are linked.

My rapidly growing knowledge enhanced my ability to further refine our program services and raised many new questions. Since the gateway into the program was fathers participating in weekly father's support groups, I developed a clinical structure for group facilitation that enabled enrolled fathers to objectively explore their maternal and paternal pasts. Finally, rounding out the program's structural components was my ability to use educational materials to enhance fathers' understanding of child development. The Partnership for A Healthy Baby – Home Visiting curriculum was one of many resources we used to educate fathers on how to appropriately respond to and support their child's development.

In summary, having supervisory and organizational support at the highest level is essential. A program structure grounded in regulatory guidelines, e.g., performance standards, emphasizing a comprehensive approach linking fathers to wraparound services is also key. An inherent belief in men's ability to invest in a process that enhances their knowledge and parenting practices is also important. Staff implementing the program must be committed to success and be willing to frequently modify program design and service delivery options.

Thoughtful, intentional, and ongoing research on the target population helps deepen one's understanding of fathers' intrinsic and extrinsic motivations for being involved and helps validate and/or invalidate belief systems. Finding the right curriculum and contributing to an eclectic approach to service design helps a great deal. Finally, the services must be designed specifically to address fathers' needs, and all staff involved in working with and supporting fathers must undergo a self-assessment.

The culture of parenting and childcare is predominantly female. When reaching out to and supporting male involvement, we must be clear about ways to involve fathers that support who they are, respond to their interests, and expand on the ways we know they interact with and support their children's development. It cannot, and must not, be a revised curriculum for what has proven, quantitatively or qualitatively, to work for mothers. A critical self-assessment is required of the program and the agency regarding their level of readiness to support a father involvement initiative. The administrators must be ready to invest in program evaluation to decide if the infrastructure is in place to support the initiative and whether they are willing to accommodate necessary changes.

Unfortunately, many women working in early childhood education programs like Head Start and Early Head Start have compromised histories with males, which impacts their ability to comfortably interact with and support men in the fathering role. The work and situations in which many women are placed make it easy for them to align with mothers against fathers' interests, even if it has negative implications for the child.

This is why maintaining professional boundaries and receiving good supervision is beneficial. When supporting fathers, it is essential that programs establish a relationship-based practice that supports efforts to collaborate with fathers. My thinking about this work began to crystallize after years of intense work, primarily with adolescent fathers. Much of the work was done with enrolled and community parents participating in the In-Step Early Head Start program in Queens, New York, with funding provided by the Department of Health and Human Services. What I found interesting, expanding upon the father's role or reinventing fatherhood practices, is merely revisiting fathering practices prior to industrialization, and expanding upon those roles, adapting as we have always done to meet the needs of a changing society.

The work requires practitioner reflection, since there is such variability in the goals and outcomes that programs might want to address. Based on the setting in which you are attempting to interact with and engage fathers, certain recommendations will be more relevant than others; however, it is important to consider various approaches.

For example, the needs of fathers living in urban areas will differ from those of fathers living in rural communities. I was taught to question things that did not make logical sense to me. As an undergraduate psychology major, I questioned stage theory and sought opportunities to challenge my professors when they introduced linear models as approaches to addressing specific problems. I would frequently pose a question or present a scenario that challenged what they were saying, and I would receive an insufficient response.

In the field of Psychology, there is never really a straight answer, as many of the symptoms we discussed that patients dealt with, or the theoretical frameworks we discussed to treat the problem, were not always effective. However, years later, having grown in my naivety after incorporating new knowledge into my schema, my understanding of the significance of linear processes has helped me tremendously as I think about strategies that are sustainable, contributing to growth and success at the program, staff, and participant levels. It is also important that these efforts can be replicated across programs.

The two programs I developed in New York, one in Queens and the other in the Bronx, helped more than 600 men of all ages step up and take responsibility for their children. My book *Fathering Me: A Journey into Fatherhood* and my film Fathering Me: The Long Walk Home depict fathers' hesitance, reticence, acceptance, pivots, shifts, challenges, and triumphs.

Both resources have helped practitioners better understand what informs and influences a father's ability and desire to be engaged. I am not sure if anyone has ever given thought to what we were able to accomplish in Queens and the Bronx. It took three years of research and really demanding work to get to a place where we had a formula, the secret sauce, if you will, that contributed to our success. An integral part of the secret sauce was my ability to synthesize, in a unique way, the many conversations and discussions I had with fathers, which culminated in my writing *Fathering Me: A Journey into Fatherhood*. The content, the issues we discussed in the groups, hearing the fathers' perspectives, and the things they were challenged by were so heartfelt and so complex; it took all that I had within me to hold it, then to try to process it and make sense of what had been shared.

Their sharing and responses to my deeper inquiries were filled with discoveries and insights regarding the challenges they faced just to survive as individuals.

I would be weighed down, as these conversations enhanced my knowledge and increased my effectiveness in engaging these men in deeper conversations. To be honest, my brain was working overtime to process heartfelt emotions, and there were times when I had to pull over, stop the car, take out my pen, and jot down my thoughts.

In life, we are truly fortunate when we are not only blessed with gifts but also find a way to understand, embrace, and use them. I was blessed with the ability to write poetry. The funny thing was, in those instances, my being filled with such powerful thoughts and the need to release or capture them was something I had never experienced before. And given that these groups would end late on Thursday night, I was focused on getting home to my sons after a long day's work to spend a little quality time, as these encounters not only motivated me but also reminded me that I, too, was a dedicated and committed father.

One way for me to manage this flurry of competing priorities was to jot down my thoughts in the form of poems. They were initially meant to help me reflect, organize my thoughts, and devise strategies for how I would continue to share key insights with these men. One day, I decided to read a poem to the group. To my astonishment, the fathers not only resonated with the poem, but they also liked the way I synthesized our process.

They wanted to hear more, so it wasn't long before I was leveraging my gift, utilizing the poems in a variety of ways — as ice breakers for professionals in the field who wanted to learn how to engage fathers, during sensitivity training for organizations, and of course, during conversations with fathers and in group sessions as appropriate.

Another eye-opening fact was that I discovered many of the individuals attending my fatherhood trainings were hesitant to engage in the conversation to begin with.

It was bewildering at first, and I did not fully understand what was happening. However, upon further observation and discussion with my team, it became clear there was not only an apparent reluctance to engage in the conversation but also genuine fear. I get it, discussing any parent-child relationship can be riddled with emotion; however, what surprised me most was that these were individuals who stated they were committed to working with fathers, and yet, they had inherent fears, hesitance, and reticence when it came to participating in these conversations in a meaningful way.

This experience helped me understand that, although we are sometimes well-intentioned, when we have not adequately dealt with our own parenting challenges, we might not be in the best position to help others. Using poems as icebreakers during these discussions and trainings depersonalized the experience, which enabled attendees to engage in meaningful conversations. It is important to reiterate that these were programs and organizations that stated they were interested in enhancing their capacity to do the work and had brought me in as an expert in the field to help them. If I were to frame their behavior as high-level skepticism, one would say I was being very generous.

I quickly realized people are fearful of confronting emotions, whether painful, pleasant, real, or imagined, if they have not adequately dealt with the advent of those emotions. Having them do so might, if you will, awaken demons and, in some respects, force them to come into close kinship with emotions they protected or buried. The ability to appropriately deal with protected emotions is an essential part of the self-assessment I talk about. If they are going to properly equip themselves to work with and engage men, this is necessary. And while it might be an arduous process, individuals who are willing to invest will become better practitioners.

When I shared my experience, background, and philosophical approach to the work, and some of our successes, I began to see tensions subside. The poems were easy to comprehend, inspirational, profound, and visually stimulating, making it easy for participants to connect and project. I saw emerging curiosity, a little less skepticism, and, based upon the head nods, a couple of potential advocates in the room. This was evidenced by their posture, looks on their faces, and questions they asked as they were intent on obtaining clarity. Others just wanted to add to the conversation.

Personalities that were dormant surfaced. I recognized the individual in the audience who possessed a certain level of expertise, waiting for the opportune moment to pounce upon any mistake I made.

There often is an advocate who is proud and happily surprised that I understand the work and that I'm truly invested in helping fathers become more accountable. My stories, the examples I share, let them into my soul, and they embrace me as one of their own. They open up, become more curious, and they ask questions, wanting to know how and why, as they are now locked in and paying attention. They are craving more, and as the presentation progresses, they are sold on the fact that I have a sound body of knowledge. I am suddenly credible, so they take risks asking more insightful questions like:

"Is it possible to replicate the program; what you've done; is it possible for you and your team to come to my organization and provide staff development training for our program leadership and individual team members?"

The session, content, the poems, and the way it was delivered contributed to increased engagement, winning them over, which affords them opportunities to share their views, dialogue with other participants, and reflect on their new learning. Just when they want more, time runs out. The presentation ends, and I am now seen as someone with considerable expertise and the capacity to convey and transfer some of that knowledge. They are thankful that I did not push too hard or challenge them to shed their defenses. The process is something to see, and as someone deeply immersed in these experiences, I always viewed them as a blessing from God. Being able to convey knowledge to practitioners, resulting in their understanding of the need to conduct a self-assessment, so they can be intentionally different as they attempt to engage with fathers, is the goal, which is a win for us all.

I have not shared this broadly; however, it is appropriate to share it now. These insights contributed to some of our foundational successes and to our engagement in a research project that firmly crystallized our approach to working with and supporting fathers, resulting in From Theory to Practice: *An Evidence-Based Model of Father Engagement.*

The research and evaluation led to the creation of a conceptual framework transferable across programs that increases the likelihood of program success if the framework is implemented with fidelity. The framework enabled us to better understand what contributed to our success, where we needed to make tweaks, and where we needed to devote time and resources, helping our entire team embrace the idea that we all needed to commit to creating a culture of inclusion, which enhanced service provision. The initial step of the conceptual model begins by having staff understand the importance of self-assessment to learn strategies that enable them to work with fathers differently.

They must go from a place where they are ineffective in communicating with fathers to one where they can communicate effectively in a variety of situations. It is not just their initial understanding and ability to do so, but also their capacity to interact with fathers on multiple levels, while sustaining communication.

This speaks to varying levels of commitment to overcoming their own challenges, seizing the moment, and taking advantage of opportunities to learn more about the fathers to better understand how to provide support for children.

It is acknowledging that they may have to confront and address gender and/or value issues, and to be careful not to influence parenting decisions based on their ideas about what is right or appropriate. Working with female staff, I observed, and their own testimonies confirm that they automatically align with the mom when there are problems in a relationship, and they admit having to work backwards to find a neutral stance before they can effectively intervene.

One way of helping staff with this issue is through individual supervision and professional development. There must be patience and an understanding that they will evolve over time during real life encounters with their colleagues and fathers.

Creating opportunities to microscopically analyze and discuss these situations helps them understand why one intervention or approach succeeded and another failed. What we quickly learn is that this is challenging work, which is why so many people avoid doing it this way. When we get this right, however, with regard to the staff, we are helping them reconstruct their approach to interacting with fathers.

We are equipping them with the skills to think on their feet, raising the professional development bar, and empowering them to have more thoughtful interactions with fathers and to bring intentionality to each encounter. We are providing support while also asking them to become increasingly comfortable with complexity.

A word of caution: it takes a lot of skill and thoughtfulness to begin uncovering layers of healthy and sometimes unhealthy defense mechanisms that have built up over time, enabling victimized individuals to heal, to function, and to function while still healing.

Evaluating whether certain defense mechanisms can or should be tinkered with requires a lot of careful observation and consideration. It is also important to recognize that, when supporting staff through the self-assessment process, issues that surface may be better served in an external therapeutic environment, which can be accessed through an agency's employee assistance program.

Another important aspect of creating a culture of inclusion is having fathers who are comfortable in the environment, come to the program on their own terms, obtain support in defining fathering practices that work for them, and are responsive to their children's developmental needs. It also helps to ensure fathers understand, as previously shared, their intrinsic and extrinsic motivations.

With this renewed or enhanced understanding, fathers are better prepared to do some of the individual work necessary for continuing growth and development, which may require individual counseling, educational and vocational linkages, and further historical explorations of their relationship or lack thereof with their fathers, which is inextricably linked to their present fathering practices. Without successfully passing through this stage, moving on to truly expanding one's definition and understanding of the ever-changing needs of their children and partners will be challenging, to say the least.

Helping fathers see the benefit of volunteering in the program if the opportunity exists, working as paid staff, or contributing to the ongoing viability of the program, helping other fathers in ways they were helped might not happen if they are not able to successfully address their individual challenges, which are connected to intrinsic values identified during the assessment stage. I will now go a little deeper into the specific steps of the framework.

Step 1. Creating a Culture of Inclusion

Practitioners who are thoughtful about their desire to design and implement appropriate services for fathers might consider some of this information akin to fatherhood 101. Creating a father-friendly environment is an important initial step that must be achieved with program staff, mothers, and the program environment.

Staff must "buy-in" to a shared philosophical approach to engage fathers. They may need to explore past experiences that could impact their interactions with fathers, and they must receive ongoing training and support to work with fathers. Mothers should also be educated about the benefits of father engagement and have any concerns about the program's approach to supporting fathers' involvement addressed. Program operations (e.g., schedules, forms) should be examined to assess father-friendliness.

It is also important to consider whether male staff are needed for outreach to fathers. In addition, the program's physical environment should include father-friendly print material and pictures. When this is done, it helps program staff engage the individual sitting in front of them. This structure helps fathers define their role in ways that matter to them.

What additional skills do you require? What else would you need? What are the obstacles?

I hope that much of the information will be familiar and it will ring true in a way that complements your thinking. While this is viewed as the initial step in the assessment process, there is so much more that must happen before one gets to this place.

I cannot stress enough how important it is to dedicate the right amount of time to contextualizing the work, understanding your population, knowing the issues, and knowing where you want to go with your efforts. It is also important to be kind to yourself and your team, as true lasting success is going to take time, so it is important to be patient with the process.

The internal focus on professional development and assessing staff's level of readiness to even take on the task of engaging fathers requires considerable attention and care. Consideration must also be given to many of the historical experiences of the population you intend to serve. There will be clinical issues that must be addressed, and cognitive processes will help staff think about fathers, recognize the need to adapt to cultural trends, and understand the implications of those changes within subcultures.

Staff development and training – Creating a Culture of Inclusion begins with an internal evaluation of an agency or organization's ability and level of readiness to provide services for fathers. Initial consideration must focus on evaluating whether the organizational structure supports the work to be done and aligns with the agency's agenda and mission. Funding streams and outcome measures dictate priorities for agencies, and so thought must be given to how these services support the agency's agenda. The personnel interacting with fathers must not only understand and support the agenda, but also be willing to participate in processes that assess their historical experiences with men – past and present. This is essential as many "family support programs" interested in involving fathers and other significant males in their children's lives are staffed primarily by women.

Programs have become more savvy about the need for a male staff member who is trained and will interact directly with the men. This is not to suggest that women cannot effectively coordinate programs or interact with men; however, women in the agency who will have any direct or indirect contact with men must conduct that self-assessment regarding their ability to engage effectively. Management and supervisory staff must be equipped and willing to provide ongoing staff development and training, demonstrating how to effectively connect with and engage fathers, as well as how to support their continued involvement. Follow-up training is also essential, as this will be an evolving process.

When I facilitated staff development training sessions, issues arose for employees that indicated the need for additional support, some of which crossed into a more personal arena, which supported my earlier reference to leveraging support from an employee assistance program. Of course, referrals are never made without the employee's knowledge or consent, as they are merely recommendations.

Environmental considerations – The programs' physical environments and print materials must be responsive to fathers and encourage their involvement. Pictures of fathers positively interacting with their children in functional roles, feeding, or changing diapers, educational opportunities, such as reading or counting together, or gross motor activity, such as outdoor physical play spaces, are nice illustrations. Waiting areas consisting of quiet spaces for fathers to decompress, providing access to social media, and a place to check emails and send messages would be ideal. Books and magazines covering topics of interest to fathers could also be placed in waiting areas where fathers might sit. Programs that are successful in creating this culture of inclusion recognize that these modifications are made with great intentionality and are not merely extensions or expansions of pre-existing services, nor are they replicas of program designs used to serve mothers.

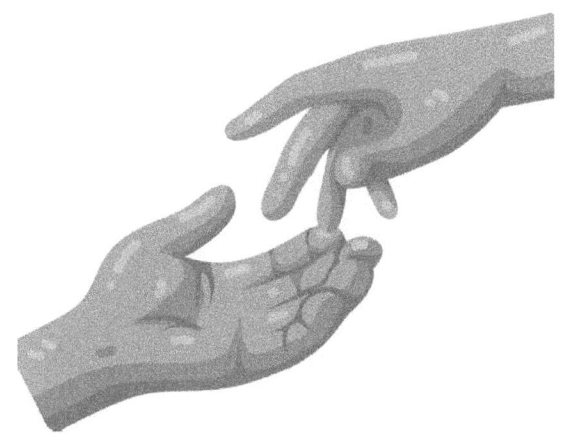

Step 2. Initializing Contact

The second component of the conceptual framework assumes programs understand the targeted population and have discussed strategies for conducting community outreach. Factors influencing the extent to which programs recruit fathers to participate in services and the outreach strategies one chooses are available funding, the agency's mission, and specific outcome measures.

Both passive, i.e., fathers coming to the program of their own volition or through referrals, and active outreach, i.e., staff approaching fathers where they gather through such means as street canvassing, visiting barbershops and basketball courts, going to local high schools, and conducting home visits, should be used to engage fathers. All program staff must operate from the position that fathers are present, available, and interested in participating, because, unless they are incarcerated, deceased, or prohibited from initiating contact due to a court order, there is potential for engagement. I would argue that if they reside in another state, they are usually also interested in being part of their child's life; they just have a few more obstacles in their way.

MAX's Story

Max enrolled in the Fathers First Program in 2001. I was invited to a home visit to meet him as part of the program's outreach efforts, and I found him to be a genuinely nice young man. After talking with him for a while, he disclosed that he was the younger brother of a father I had met back in 1995, when I was supporting the In-Step Program. The conversation jarred my memory, and I immediately remembered his older brother as an equally solid young man. I was looking forward to working with Max. He was confident, focused, and seemed to be in a good place regarding the pregnancy. I did not have to do a lot of convincing, as my former relationship with his brother gave me a little street credit.

However, Max did not immediately engage in program services beyond the home visits. He found employment as a security guard, so he was earning money to provide for his child.

At 16, he started boxing as an amateur, and in 1998, he won the Daily News Golden Gloves. At the time, he was 19 years old, training for a spot on the 2000 U.S. Olympic boxing team, when he found out he was going to be a father. The distraction was too much, and he fell short of his quest to become an Olympian. He would later share that he was overwhelmed at the thought of becoming a father.

His participation in the Fathers First program eventually increased, and staff within the program helped him realize he had a new priority: his son. He made the difficult decision to place his dreams on hold, hanging up his gloves to embrace his new responsibility.

Max dedicated all his efforts to learning how to be a good father and provider. When his son was six months of age, the child's mother took the baby to North Carolina and did not return. Max was dumbfounded and did not understand why she had left or why she was not planning to return. She discontinued all communication, which he thought was strange. He had done everything, given up his dream, got a job, moved the young lady into his home to live with him and his parents, and it still was not enough.

I guided Max through the process of filing a court petition to obtain visitation rights. We were successful in submitting the petition. This took a lot of cross-state communication and collaboration. The mother initially refused to comply, so we helped him file a contempt petition, and she was eventually forced to return to New York for a court hearing. Max was advised to obtain a paternity test, and the results revealed that the child was not his biological son.

He was devastated that he had been misled. He spiraled, lost focus, lost his job, and engaged in behaviors that were self-defeating. This went on for several months, and although he maintained his connection to the program, he participated in individual sessions more than in support groups. One day, during an individual session, I asked him when he was most happy in life.

When did he feel like he was truly in control of his life and the decisions he was making? His response was when he was boxing. That was when he took the necessary steps to begin training to enter the Golden Gloves again.

Max was well-known in the New York boxing circuit. Many of the officials were happy to see that he was back in the ring. And although he put up a valiant effort, he was eliminated in the semi-finals. I was there, I saw the fight, and it was clear that the judges robbed him. They were focused on his younger opponent, whom they felt had a promising future. It did not matter because Max was so encouraged by his performance that he decided he wanted to turn professional. I was instrumental in helping him make the decision.

He returned to the gym, trained hard, took the necessary steps to get in shape, and in July of 2004, he returned to boxing as a professional. "The Damager" (his fight name) made his professional debut at the Orange County Fairgrounds on October 30th, in Middletown, NY. He fought on the card alongside John Duddy, who eventually became a champion. They both trained at the Irish Ropes Boxing Club in Arverne, NY. Max's paternity situation derailed his career and robbed him of the opportunity to become an Olympic athlete, which was unfortunate. I am sad to say situations like these occur too frequently. Establishing relationships with community partners and knowing how to navigate and utilize services to help fathers when confronted with difficult situations is key.

***

Community needs assessments and statistical data of the targeted community are essential sources of information about challenges residents face, which will have a direct impact on a programs outreach efforts, the methods programs choose and directly connects to whether more emphasis should be placed on active vs passive outreach.

It is important to realize, many well-intended programs without extensive histories outreaching to males will rely on the adage,

"If we build it, meaning a program, they will come," which is an ineffective passive approach.

This misconception frequently results in agency frustration with understanding why fathers are unresponsive to recruitment efforts, limiting program success in this area. It is also useful to remember that programs providing services to families, primarily women and children, historically excluded men and were not equipped to deal with them effectively. Trust is difficult to establish when working with a population who from a historical perspective have not only been excluded but denied opportunity.

Therefore, understanding how to utilize relationships established with other community-based organizations can be a great source of outreach. These other programs, in many instances, share a similar philosophical approach to servicing clients. They are concerned about the same issues, which is why you partnered with them in the first place. Sharing information about your program, hours of operations, events, and providing them with an abundance of your marketing materials for their clients are other ways programs can expand their outreach, i.e., creating websites, and connecting on social media.

The degree to which you educate community partners about your service delivery model increases their capacity to educate others that the services your program provides are valuable and unique. Especially if fathers are benefiting from the services you provide, your community partners will advertise for you.

Step 3. Relationship Building

Communication, collaboration, patience, reflection, and trust building are key ingredients in relationship development with fathers, and they should be the cornerstone of interactions between program staff and participants.

From the onset, fathers should be informed of the program's purpose and how the program can benefit them and their children. Judgmental interactions should be avoided by focusing on the father's strengths, what he is already doing, which is positive, and how it can serve as his foundation in his development as a father. Providing targeted services and the way fathering is defined within an agency both impact the type of relationships staff will choose to develop with fathers.

These decisions drive expectations and correlate to our success or failures when it comes to interacting with and supporting fathers in their roles to define fathering practices that are palatable for them. Many times, what they are initially able and willing to give may not meet our expectations.

The relationships we establish with fathers must begin with an expanded definition of fatherhood that explores and respects the fact that, just because we cannot visually observe interactions between fathers and their children, it does not necessarily mean they are nonexistent. It does not mean fathers are disinterested or uninvolved. There are critical aspects of parenting practices that are culturally specific, and aspects of parenting practices that are unobservable, which in many instances can inform and influence what your relationship and area of focus with a father will be.

I am talking about cognitive, affective, and behavioral demonstrations that are essential to a child's everyday survival but do not fit in so nicely with our schematic of what involvement or engagement looks like. Relationships begin with respectful, patient communication and with exploratory questions. Beginning on some common ground or point of interest, even if it is nothing more than providing fathers with additional information about your program and its mission to work with fathers, is a good place to start.

If we were to pay close attention, there is a parallel process in how we develop relationships with children who enter our programs through the Department of Children and Family Services, Family Court, home, or center-based programs, juxtaposed to the relationships we develop with fathers. Practitioners approach children with patience and caution, effectively assessing their comfort levels and their needs.

Over time, as mutual comfort increases, the relationships evolve. Children grow in their ability to communicate their needs to us as they become more familiar and comfortable with the environment, who we are, and how we show up.

Fathers, although equipped with varying levels of skill in effectively communicating their needs, will only do so when they believe we are truly invested in collaborating with them, sharing experiences, and providing them with timely and relevant information they can use to change their circumstances. When we are patient and allow time for trust building, and we support fathers' self-identified goals, we can demonstrate, through non-judgmental feedback and dialogue, our levels of acceptance of their progress or lack thereof, without it influencing the relationship.

This is a deeper level of connectedness and sustained engagement than many of us have prepared for or have experienced in the past. I recognize that it is easy to see the need for this type of commitment when it comes to children; however, we often lose sight of it when we think about our interactions and engagement with fathers.

Step 4. Assessments

Assessing each father's priorities is essential when building trust and eliciting their "buy-in" to the program. While an early childhood program's primary purpose may be to optimize child development, parents' individual needs must first be addressed. Many inexperienced fathers often require staff's assistance when planning & plotting the steps needed to achieve their goals.

After a roadmap for the father's development is established based on his needs and motivations, the father and program staff can develop priorities for which actions to pursue and in what order.

Now, let us engage in a discussion of motivations and how they influence a father's engagement. We can only adequately assess what we have taken the time to observe and learn more about. Our relationships, when solid, lead to a deeper understanding of what motivates fathers to be fathers. If our observations are thoughtful and intentional, we can identify strengths in individuals, assess how they can use these strengths to support their development, and, at the same time, identify and discuss behaviors that limit their success. With this type of insight, they can begin to embrace the need for change and support their increased understanding of this evolutionary process of fatherhood. The notion of becoming a father is linked to identity formation. This is where past learning experiences and methods of responding to challenging situations evolve over time. Self-regulation in males is something that the social system expects.

Not only does society expect it, but it mandates it in some spaces and places and dictates it in others. We even expect infants and toddlers to learn at an early age how to self-regulate. It is essential that we find ways to help them understand this critical aspect of development.

Accordingly, fathers tend to respond to threatening or disrespectful situations by drawing on reactive behaviors necessary for survival in some settings but frowned upon in others. The conflict is that in some communities, a subculture exists where fathers reside, and making the choice not to regulate behavior is typical. Programs that are well-intentioned, seeking to provide essential services, enter disenfranchised communities with the goal, in many instances, of strongly influencing behavior change based on what is deemed acceptable by the dominant culture.

In many instances, this contradicts learned ways of being that are necessary for survival within these subcultures. You get no argument from me that this is a daunting task. The need for fathers to modify their behavior, commonly referred to and experienced as conformity, is important for them to understand and embrace if they are going to grow as individuals and as parents. The program's agenda can then address many of the extrinsic needs of fathers by providing essential information around parenting knowledge, as well as providing opportunities for them to practice newly learned skills.

A young father shared, "The second I found out I was becoming a parent, I panicked and did not know what to do.
The father's program helped a lot, teaching me to be patient
and providing me with essential information. I also had to
change how I responded to situations. I am Puerto Rican, and
it is my experience that fathers do not really get respect here
in America. I first encountered this discrimination when my
daughter's mom went into labor. They did not even ask me if
I wanted to go into the delivery room. They acted like I was
not even there. Normally, when I am disrespected in this way,
I usually go off and put people in their place. The program
helped me to analyze situations for what they are and then try
to control my response so that I do not sabotage my ability to
get something that my family desperately needs." J. Santiago

Life management skills such as the one just described are essential
and are translatable to many situations that fathers will find
themselves in, such as obtaining gainful employment, which is
always a goal. The decision to assist a father with employment or
to help them secure more suitable employment is an achievable
goal. Level of readiness becomes an important consideration
and an essential question as many fathers enter programs saying
they want a job, need a job, and they expect the program to help
because they believe employment will solve all their problems.
Many fathers are concerned about paying child support, securing
better housing, meeting their basic necessities, getting suitable
transportation, and more. It is important to help them recognize
that the unmet needs of their child and family have existed for

some time before your engagement with them, and that they cannot be erased overnight.

Addressing immediate expressed concrete needs is important. It is also important to consider the possibility that programs might be setting fathers up for failure and adversely impacting on-going work with them in the future. For example, if I had a sneaky suspicion that a father's goals conflict with reality, or if they were not ready to take on a particular task, I'd attempt to explore this with them and help them evaluate whether their goals need refinement. This often contradicts our desire and need to respond to their immediate needs. However, it is critically important to ascertain whether our meeting that particular need will be a temporary solution to an immediate problem or will expose the need for soft skills and job-readiness training.

Step 5. Prioritizing Action Steps

Fathers should be encouraged to start with a goal that is easily attainable, as this will set a precedent for success. It is important for us, as helping professionals, to recognize that we navigate neighborhoods that are under-resourced and dangerous, which makes us feel uncomfortable as we travel through them.

If this is our experience, imagine what it must feel like for fathers to live there and not be able to escape to a more promising neighborhood or the suburbs. This is how one young father described his experience growing up in Far Rockaway, which at one point in time was considered one of the most violent communities in New York.

"The biggest thing about coming into fatherhood is you are not sure what family is all about, especially if you grew up in Rockaway, in a dysfunctional family. You have no idea what a good man is or how to raise a family. You are still trying to find your place in society, finish school, and find a job. You feel like you cannot do anything for the child anyway. What gave me comfort is Mr. Jones, who helped to reinforce that everything was going to be alright." D. Hooper

How important are engagement strategies when it comes to helping a father prioritize his goals?

Once we discover who this father is and a little about his motivations, and he understands or is clear about his role as a father, programs can further assist in conceptualizing his interests and begin to collaboratively prioritize action steps. Outlining specific opportunities for goal attainment and sustained involvement in their child's life is key. The conceptual model begins with fathers who are comfortable in the environment, come to the program on their own terms, obtain support in defining fathering practices that work for them, and are supportive of their children's development. Finally, conversations with fathers about their interests lead to a greater understanding of their intrinsic and extrinsic motivations. As a result of this renewed understanding of self, fathers are better prepared to do some of the individual work necessary for continuing growth and development, which may involve individual counseling, educational and vocational training, and further historical explorations of their relationship or lack thereof with their own fathers, which is inextricably linked to their current fathering practices. When fathers fail to embrace their responsibility, single mothers often raise children. If mothers are unable to move beyond the fractured relationship or the broken promises, and they still have anger towards the father, it might manifest as conscious or unconscious bias towards the child. A mother's unresolved trauma may interfere with her ability to sensitively respond to her infant, thus affecting the development of a healthy attachment to her own child. Many mothers have difficulty regulating their emotions, leading to outbursts of anger or frustration, especially when dealing with their child's emotional needs. Some mothers become overly protective, fearing repeating the trauma they experienced, while others may become emotionally detached or neglectful. Trauma can also alter a mother's perception of her child, leading to harsher judgments and a diminished ability to see the child's positive qualities.

It can make it difficult for mothers to set appropriate boundaries with their children, either by being overly permissive or excessively controlling. Others unconsciously project their own fears and insecurities onto their children, leading to unhealthy patterns of interaction. The cycle of trauma can perpetuate through generations, as mothers pass on their unresolved trauma to their children, creating a pattern of unhealthy attachment and parenting.

Understanding the impact parents can have on their children supports the notion that this model is linear in many respects because, without successfully passing through this stage, moving on to truly expand one's definition of fatherhood, and understanding the ever-changing needs of their children, responsive fathering will be challenging, if not impossible.

"The things I learned here are unbelievable. It is not like children come with instructions. I thought you take them to the park, get them ice cream, and read with them. I did not think I had to help with homework. If I worked outside of the home, and paid the rent, then my job was done. I thought my wife was happy doing that stuff."

D. McNeil

Helping fathers see the benefit of volunteering in the program if the opportunity exists, working as paid staff or contributing to the on-going viability of the program supporting other fathers in ways they benefited will not happen if they cannot successfully address their individual challenges, which are connected to intrinsic values identified through their individual assessment.

Step 6. Engagement Strategies

Opportunities for father involvement should be diverse, occurring at the individual, familial (with child and/or mother), program, and community levels. Many programs offer limited options for fathers to get involved and should, if possible, expand opportunities.

If the range of engagement opportunities aligns with fathers' interests, program participation will be greater. Poets impress me with their ability to connect with and influence the thought processes of individuals from diverse backgrounds with varying ethnic, social, and political positions, helping them find common ground. And yet, they offer individual and collective insights into issues that lend themselves to interpretation based on historical experiences, cognitive capacity, and an openness to enlightened thinking.

This model/approach to service delivery is poetic in that it provides parameters for expanded definitions of fatherhood while simultaneously defining ways for fathers to find meaning in the parenting journey and also better understand themselves.

The parallel process is that practitioners, in a similar fashion, are asked to assess themselves and their intervention methods, motivations, and sustained investment in doing this work, in a manner that lends itself to growth for them as well. All the wisdom in the world could not have prepared me for what to expect or for how to appreciate at the time, or for how pivotal I became to many of the fathers I encountered over the years.

This self-investment and willingness to connect, becoming something for someone that does not initially have identifiable characteristics, is risky. I provided a corrective experience for many of these men, fathering some, coaching some, and mentoring others, in addition to creating within them the expectation that professionals could be helpful by being real. My team and I joined fathers on their journey as they identified and refined their goals, scaffolded their knowledge, and engaged with their children in developmentally appropriate ways.

This was done through individual sessions, support groups, crisis intervention, advocacy, and referrals to legal assistance. And, when they were ready, we supported their personal and professional development.

By no means am I suggesting that we had all the requisite expertise that was needed to assist these men; however, my team members and I were skillful at connecting them to trusted, sensitive, responsive professionals who were going to listen intently and help them take ownership of addressing their needs. This reminds me of one final point: how important it is for organizations to establish partnerships and/or memorandums of understanding with organizations that share a similar philosophical approach to supporting families, and in particular, working with fathers.

An Evidenced Based Model of Father Engagement

Engagement Phase Fathers' First Evidence-Based Model

1) Creating a Culture of Inclusion
   a. Shared philosophical approach
   b. Professional Development & Training
   c. Self-assessment

2) Initializing Contact
   a. Outreach & Recruitment
   b. Reaching Out
   c. Community Partners
   d. MOU's

3) Relationship Building
   a. Authentic Conversations
   b. Collecting historical data
   c. Self-disclosure
   d. Defining the working relati

4) Assessment
   a. Intrinsic Motivations
   b. Extrinsic Motivations

5) Prioritizing Action Steps
   a. Goal setting
   b. Connecting to resources

6) Engagement Strategies
   a. Programmatic Investments
   b. Referrals
   c. Additional Support Services

I never gave much thought to how industrialization has informed, influenced, and shaped parenting practices. What is clear, as a result of changes in family configurations, family dynamics, and schedules, cohabitating couples need to make arrangements that eradicate gender prescribed roles when it comes to childcare, child rearing, and the associated responsibilities of maintaining a home. This shift has caused us to ask more from fathers. Of course, I am stating the obvious when I share that there is a universal problem of fatherlessness in America that crosses all ethnicities and socioeconomic statuses. The fatherlessness I am speaking of is a lack of appropriate and consistent involvement in a child's life that affects all the developmental domains that we in early childhood education are concerned about, as it relates to supporting children's development.

In my work, I have focused on low-income fathers, primarily African American and Latino males. This was due in part to a subjective experience but more so to the pain of observing children in marginally underserved communities who were failing to thrive. What do I mean when I say failing to thrive? I am not using the term in the typical sense, suggesting they were not meeting essential medical and or developmental milestones. What I am referring to is their confidence, self-esteem, and belief in their capacity to accomplish, achieve, and be successful in life. What was more interesting to me was that no one seemed to notice or care. In my observation, these young boys and men were expendable. So, it should not surprise you when I share that I felt vindicated when I met with success almost immediately, engaging young men and designing services to address their pressing needs. As I embarked upon this journey, I attributed my success to my humility and my ability to take my emerging expertise and fuse it with the father's understanding of their own experience. I can honestly say, I did not truly understand how I knew; however, I became aware that once they fully understood their own experiences, places and places where they could have made different decisions, or where they did not receive the requisite support, they had a responsibility to try and fill the gaps, by focusing on outstanding tasks that would make them whole. Things like obtaining their GED or High School diploma, getting criminal records expunged, complying with anger management, or parenting classes. All of this is necessary if they are to carve out a better life for themselves and create a different experience for their children. It is important to add that helping fathers with this required considerable diplomacy, as many did not immediately see how improving their own lives would positively influence their children's outcomes.

As I sit here pondering over what I am writing, it seems and sounds overly simplistic; however, I found that to be the case. The investment was grounded in a commodity we are all running out of, which is time. True authentic investments, the ones that garner the most results, are meaningful, respectful, intentional, targeted investments focused on helping those who are willing to allow us to help. This is what our fathers, children, and families require.

The question becomes, what is our charge? Is it to define the meaning of father engagement? Is that our charge really, or is that a distinct, and uniquely individualized decision fathers must make? Are we attempting to define and decide appropriate fathering practices? Everything done in relation to caring for and providing for children can be couched under the umbrella of parenting practices, which is an important part of the father's role today. Embedded in this conversation is a need to consistently enhance one's parenting competency. And at the same time, we must acknowledge that there are many ways to succeed in our parenting endeavors, so we must be patient and flexible. It is also important that we expose and work to change practices we know are damaging or harmful to children.

Organizations delivering early childhood services, when hiring staff, must assess and evaluate whether there are any biases towards men or whether they have issues working with men. Professional development training must evaluate the benefits of creating environments that enable men to be employed. This places them in situations where they can be instrumental supporting fathers, if they are willing to do so.

An awareness of the impact that mothers' gatekeeping can have on organizational culture is also key. Most often, when mothers gatekeep, they are not intentionally attempting to keep fathers out of the child's life. They are uninformed and sometimes hold on to unimaginably painful feelings about challenges in the current and/or past relationship. They are unable or unwilling to let go of hurt feelings.

A 2022 report from Fatherhood.org indicated that 17% of mothers wished their spouse were more involved, while 40% of fathers felt their child's mother was interfering with their involvement.

In my experience, most mothers want their child's father to positively engage with the child or children they share. Although studies show that some mothers may not actively encourage or facilitate this involvement, it is incumbent upon programs to help mothers understand and appreciate the benefits for them and their children when fathers are positively engaged. Mothers are often saddled with so much responsibility while caring for their children that they don't have time for themselves or to recognize their unmet needs. If we can help fathers accept and embrace their fathering responsibilities, it creates opportunities for mothers to focus on their unmet goals. Goals that were temporarily disrupted because of the pregnancy. This is one of the methods we used to explain to mothers when they pushed back or expressed concerns about our focus on fathers, that there were potential benefits for the entire family if we were able to increase the father's engagement. Research consistently demonstrates that children with engaged fathers are more likely to succeed academically, experience fewer behavioral problems, and have greater overall well-being.

———————————~··~————————

Surviving The Test

Commitment often goes beyond what the job normally entails.

I am in unique company when I share that I have been in the trenches, caring about, focused on, and committed to changing the plight of young African American boys and men for decades. What began with a focus on adolescent boys turned into a desire to help prepare young fathers for the important developmental trajectory we have come to refer to as fatherhood. What was also unique about my experience, my journey, if you will, is that it was fathers who ended up being the target population. The area where I had the greatest impact, where I made my mark, was when I started a program to support teenage mothers.

So, again, it is my hope that Making the Case: Intentional Father Engagement will help practitioners understand what they need to consider if they seriously want to work with and support fathers. Many of these considerations, the things I am recommending, which can increase the likelihood of success when interacting with and engaging fathers, are not necessarily new. In fact, the skill in effectively and efficiently utilizing these strategies, or better yet, considerations, will be in leveraging existing knowledge, rethinking your current orientation, and training, based upon what your discipline allows, and nuancing conversations with recipients of services to ensure you are meeting them on a parallel ground.

And while this might sound like an oversimplification of complex work, I invite you to embark on this journey with me. I am curious what the world's reaction would be if I were to author a book on motherhood. As an African American male who never mothered a soul, can I accurately address, even on a foundational level, what the job entails? It would be difficult to do, given my experiences and view of the world.

I have navigated life through the eyes of a man, so writing about the experiences of doing so as a woman would put me at a distinct disadvantage. I am confident in sharing that, as a clinician, there were even times when it was difficult for me to work with female clients, which had nothing to do with me but more with their comfort level discussing certain topics with me. And yet, individuals who are grounded in privilege, operating from the position of a researcher or some feigned authority, have authored books on fathers and what I refer to as the fatherhood journey for years, receiving too much critical acclaim.

When I talk about the fatherhood journey, I am talking about the place where I live, have lived, and have learned many lessons along the way in my efforts to support others in this role. Most fathers must accept responsibility and ease their fears by understanding what it means to be willing to live in an uncomfortable place and work diligently to grow every day, increasing their knowledge as they learn and adapt to the responsibility.

These authors, however, are speaking from what they suggest is personal experience, voicing their opinion about what works best when engaging fathers, yet they have never been in that position. And while well-intentioned, I am not so sure they can adequately capture the essence of the experience (as researchers and spectators) when much of what they know, see, and observe is vicarious.

As a clinician in my work with young women, although I have been known to be quite effective in my interactions, assessments, recommendations, and treatment, I recognize quite clearly that there are places where I cannot effectively go without the counsel of some of my female colleagues.I am not privileged, I have never been, and I doubt I ever will be. Now, I admit, I have been the benefactor of guidance and support, which completely changed the trajectory of my life. I have found a way to successfully navigate society by going to school to obtain an advanced degree. This was done so I could position myself to have an impact on others, in ways that the system helped me when I was a child. I had to come to terms with the pitfalls and traps that existed in society for men with a particular hue; men who looked like me.

I learned how to successfully navigate said pitfalls and make conscious decisions every day. What I bring to the table that is different is that, although I have been the benefactor of unique opportunities, rising from the ashes of poverty and loss, when it comes to working with this targeted population, one of the factors that contributes to my success is that I'm tangible when it comes to these men, fathers, and their families. They are able to relate to me because I am seen as one of them.

I am an African American male. I grew up in poverty. I navigated and resided in marginalized communities. I worked at the grassroots level. I have provided direct services, designing and developing programs focused on their needs. My goal in helping others was to give back in hopes that the fathers would be able to translate the knowledge and skills they developed into their fathering practices.

A bonus would be for them to care about and invest in their community as well. I am not only one of them, but I will forever be viewed in that light if I am authentic. What is it that we mean when we reference being authentic? It means being genuine, real, someone who lives their life according to their own beliefs, goals, and values, rather than those of other people or the greater society. I, like so many others, found a way to work within the system, and yet the system does not dictate how I choose to live my life or engage. I am an independent thinker, and I do what is expected, not necessarily always following a playbook.

During a recent presentation for Strong Starts Court Initiative, which is a Family-Court based, specialized, intergenerational collaborative approach to handling abuse and neglect cases involving children from birth to three years of age. I was introduced by an esteemed colleague as a beacon, referring to a fire or light set up in a high or prominent position as a warning signal.

Gil Foley, PhD, is a Clinical Psychologist with a depth of experience in early childhood development. He has authored and co-authored several books, and he referred to me and my work in this space as instrumental. He shared a memory of when we first met, our trajectory of getting to know each other, and the level of respect we have for each other. His reference to me as a beacon of light in a dark space, the world of fatherhood, surprised me. I was moved, and for a moment, I was lost for words. It is rare for a student to reach a level where he is on a peer level with one of his esteemed colleagues. When this happens, you know that you have arrived. What does it mean to truly arrive? It is knowledge, experience, the capacity to convey that knowledge, and, finally, admiration and respect from one's peers and former mentors.

I was told by a respected colleague that when writing about one's journey, it is important to begin at the beginning. It helps people immerse themselves in the experiences you share about your journey. What is most important is that you provide the details in a manner that makes the most sense. And while I agree, I have learned that sometimes it is important to let your audience, those who might be interested in joining you on the journey, know how it ends before you take them for a ride.

I will let you be the judge as to whether this works. At any rate, here is another part of my story. I say a part, because I am still embarking upon the journey, and I do not quite know where it is going to end. However, I believe that if you take a risk and join me, you will reap the rewards. I thought this was the culmination of my work; however, as the saying goes, tell God your plans.

Searching

Searching for the words,
one thing I'd surely say,
on the day I met my father
even though he'd gone away.

Not a chance meeting for me
it was surely planned,
I'd walk over to his car nod a while,
stick out my hand.

Our eyes would then meet
a subtle gentle stare,
with questions of acceptance,
lingering in the air.

Would I accept and forgive him
can he relate to me,
can we both put it behind us,
all the things that can never be.

I fight desperately to contain
the feelings deep down inside,
my thoughts of my dear father,
of happiness and pride.

Of special little feelings
I didn't want to show,
not sure how he would take it,
or if he even wanted to know.

Lost words did surround us
he was trying really hard,
to say something meaningful,
not something I'd disregard.

I wanted to let him off the hook yet,
didn't know what to say,
for I was equally anxious and
confused this winter day.

So, in that special moment,
the one I'd been yearning for,
I was still searching for words as
he walked away once more,
as he walked right out the door!

Fathering Me: The Long Walk Home

There is no telling how many miles you will have to run when chasing a dream.

My fatherhood journey resurrected itself with the premiere of my documentary <u>Fathering Me: The Long Walk Home</u>, being accepted into the Washington Film Festival, and the eventual screening at the World Film Fair in New York City on October 21, 2018. It was surreal as I had friends, family, former college classmates, and several colleagues who traveled from cities across the United States to join me and my team.

I did not go to film school, nor did I ever imagine I would make a film; however, life has a way of placing us exactly where we need to be when we need to be there. My professional career and a major personal life change forced me to walk away from a job that I loved. It was about five years after my departure that I noticed that practitioners, several professionals, some of whom were colleagues working in the fatherhood field, needed guidance on how to engage men in ways that provided meaningful outcomes and sustainable change. I did not think for a minute that I had all the answers; however, what I was sure of was that at the peak of my involvement in the fatherhood movement, I was making a huge difference, contributing to lasting and sustainable impacts in the lives of the men who allowed me to partner with them.

At one time, my name was synonymous with fatherhood in New York City and throughout the tri-state area. We were recruiting, enrolling, and engaging men in ways that were impressive because we focused on meaningful, lasting outcomes. I was at a fatherhood conference in Memphis, Tennessee, in 2017. I was there to present a couple of training sessions on the Office of Head Start's new Birth to Five Father Engagement Guide, a book I co-authored. Working as a federal employee, my perspective shifted from a city- and state-focused to a national focus.

Although I was not hired to lead the Office of Head Start's father engagement efforts, over time, because of my expertise, the Director, Yvette Sanchez-Fuentes, called upon me to co-lead our father engagement efforts. We had just rolled out and disseminated the resource to grant recipients across the country, and I wanted these programs, focused on engaging fathers, to be aware of and use the guide in their work with fathers.

I ran into one of my colleagues at the airport, someone I hadn't seen in a while. I respected his hustle, and I honestly believed at the time his intentions were good, and I still do; however, I think somewhere along the way, he lost focus. We were both headed to the conference, and he offered me a ride. So, instead of catching a Lyft, we rode together to the venue in his rental car. My colleague was leading the Office of Family Assistance's Training and Technical Assistance arm.

He also had his own private non-profit. The Office of Family Assistance funded many of the nation's Healthy Marriage and Responsible Fatherhood grants, so many of these agencies would be in attendance. My plan was to only be there a couple of days, and during the ride, he confirmed the same. I was curious about why he had so many bags, so I commented on the amount of luggage he was carrying, and he shared that it was camera equipment.

To my surprise, he was screening a film at the conference. He asked if I had an opportunity to stop in. Schedule permitting, he would appreciate my perspective and support. After glancing at my schedule, I confirmed that I would be able to attend. On the day of the screening, I arrived a few minutes early and took a seat in the back of the room.

By the time the screening began, at least 60 or 70 practitioners from across the country were sitting in a room, anxious to view the film. Roughly 50% of attendees were Head Start staff. I was sitting in a place of curiosity and optimism.

It was not more than 20 minutes into the film when several concerns surfaced for me regarding the content, but more importantly, the messaging. It was very self-serving on the part of the filmmaker, and it presented more of a personal story and a rationale for why he was engaged in the work, rather than anything substantial for individuals wanting to get better at engaging men and enhancing their capacity to learn what it would take. It did not address strategies for engaging men or provide examples of how men had benefited from his efforts.

The content was provocative, emotion-laden, and impactful. It was a sympathetic story about how his father was never really involved in his life and an emotional reunion, shortly prior to his father's death. There were celebrities opining on what needed to happen in programs serving fathers. A couple of mothers were at least to me forcibly emoting on the challenges of raising children without their fathers. A key message in the film focused on the difficulties men face in managing their anger.

True to form, our programs operate from a deficit model; however, this was no different from Father Billboards painting them in a negative light for their failures. It also focused immensely on fathers' pain. Although the content was relevant, it was disjointed, and important connections that could have been made were not.

The film did not provide guidance on what program staff needed to do to engage fathers in ways that resulted in meaningful outcomes. What was more disappointing was the reaction from the attendees. Based on their response, they really enjoyed the film, as I overheard discussions about their plans to use it in their programs. I walked away disappointed because, to me, the film was dangerously misleading. I made the difficult decision not to share my feedback with my colleague. Based upon my observation, he behaved as if he had nailed it.

Talking to myself, I reflected on the work I'd done in the Bronx and Queens, New York. I said in that moment, I could make a film based on our work. If I focused on highlighting and illustrating our approach to the work, the critical insights we learned from our interactions with fathers, and some of the impacts and outcomes we achieved, it might accomplish what I believe was the original intent of my colleagues' project. What these individuals, some seasoned and others not so much, needed more than anything were strategies.

So, in that moment, although I was not intricately aware, a seed had been planted, and a decision was made. Months later, as I embarked upon planning the project, I engaged colleagues, family, and friends to assess their level of interest and willingness to participate. I wanted it to be authentic, so only individuals who were invested and connected to the actual program's service delivery were invited to my planning sessions and the film project.

I told myself creating the film was my way of giving back, sharing lessons learned, and the essential tenets of what it takes to design meaningful programs for young men. I was determined to share how we helped them navigate the waters of one of the most difficult jobs a man will ever do if he invests and takes it seriously, that of being an actively engaged father. Where does one begin to conceptualize making a documentary film when they have never walked the halls of anyone's film school? Conducting research is the obvious answer, and so I did my due diligence by talking with the one and only filmmaker I knew. At least that is how I viewed him as a solid up-and-coming filmmaker. I must take you back in time a little bit to explain this further.

His name was Benjamin Norman, a photojournalist who was fortunate enough to freelance for the *New York Times*. When we met, he was a young photographer just starting out. He had done some intermittent work for the *Times*, and of course, he was hoping to do more, to get a leg up and eventually become one of their staff photographers.

I was sitting in my office when Richard Rothstein, a cool guy from our development office, called me to talk about the Bronx Fatherhood Program. He knew of this young photographer who wanted to meet me and discuss the possibility of doing a story on the program and the great work we were doing with and for young fathers.

Not one to say no too quickly, I was open to the idea, and so I told Richard to have him reach out to me. I am not sure if it was anxiety or naivety of youth; however, within seconds after hanging up the phone, it rang. It was Ben on the other line. I could tell he was young. I assumed, from his voice, that he was educated, and I sensed he was nervous. He introduced himself, asked a few questions about our model, and we agreed to meet on Thursday before father's group. Ben arrived early, and we sat down for a conversation. He told me a little more about some of the work he had done in the past, the things that interested him, and what he hoped to accomplish with me. He was cautious in telling me; he was not sure there was a story worth telling; however, he really wanted to find out. He was hoping that I would give him the opportunity. It's funny in life: sometimes you meet people and right off the bat you know this is someone I would never work with, and then there are times when you almost immediately take a liking to someone and are at least open to giving them a chance to work themselves out of that opportunity. It was the latter as it relates to Ben.

It is also important to mention that this experience was not new. Since I started the Fathers First Program in Queens, I have been approached by several prominent individuals in the film industry who have achieved a certain level of success that wanted to film a documentary about my programs. I was open to the conversation; however, I was extremely suspicious about their motivation.

The first person to approach me about making a film about the Fathers First program was Martin Bell. He was a Grammy-nominated documentarian, best known for his film Streetwise. He was referred to me by a colleague who felt the work I was doing was phenomenal, so she made the introduction.

We scheduled a meeting, and I was invited to his loft in SoHo. When I entered his living space, I shook my head in awe, thinking it must be nice. It was expansive, filled with expensive art, nice furniture, and a restaurant-style kitchen. There was a section in one corner of the room where he did some of his filming, with lights, a green screen, and a couple of massive cameras. He was very hospitable; he talked about some of the projects he was working on, referenced the film project, and, of course, shared his interest in the fathers' program. I did a little research on him and was embarrassed that I had not heard of him before; however, I was prepared for our meeting. At any rate, we had a good conversation, and I was open to the idea after his pitch. I invited him out to observe a group session and to meet with some of the fathers, and then we agreed to talk more. He arrived, met with the fathers, and left even more excited.

This was a few weeks before Max was about to have his first professional fight in upstate New York. A couple of other fathers and I promised him we would attend. Martin reached out to me and said he would love to work with me. He remembered our conversation during the group when I excitedly shared the information about Max's professional debut. Martin asked if he could tag along and film the experience, behind the scenes, and the fight. I consulted with Max, and he was open to it, so I agreed.

Martin was at the venue when we arrived, and he was able to begin filming immediately. Max was fighting on the same card as John Duddy, an Irish fighter from Londonderry, Ireland. Given that they were gym mates, there was a great deal of excitement in the room. Max put on a great show, and it seemed to me that he had done enough to pull out the win, but unfortunately, he lost by a close decision.

It was the following Monday, around 9:00 a.m., that I was sitting at my desk in the Queens office when I received a call from Martin. He was sending over a proposal and a contract outlining his plan for our work together. I told him I would review it and get back to him. I was always a little concerned when something seemed too good to be true, and after reading the proposal and scanning the contract, I felt this was the case. And because this story was not just about me, I had to discuss this with the fathers, which I did. One of the things I immediately learned was that documentary films rarely, if ever, make any money. They are human-interest stories used to shed light on important work. Attention can be instrumental in securing funding from philanthropic organizations. So, learning that was helpful. However, in the event the film proved overwhelmingly successful, the contract stipulated that we, the fathers, and I would not benefit financially in any way. Martin would have the final say on what happened with the film and its proceeds, both foreign and domestic.

That did not sit well with me. I mean, if these films never really made any money, why was it necessary to include this stipulation in the contract? When I explained this to the fathers, we collectively agreed to pass on the opportunity. When I called Martin to inform him, he tried everything within his power to convince me that this was industry standard for anyone embarking upon their first film and that if by some chance the film was successful, he would do right by me and the fathers, and yet that part was not outlined in the contract, so we decided to opt out. He would not relent, so I stopped communicating with him.

I did not regret my decision to walk away from the opportunity. I knew we were doing great work, making an impact, and garnering the attention of an entire organization, shifting the culture. Most of the staff in the organization were aware of our work. Nurses were aware of the need to take advantage of opportunities to connect with fathers. Our development office promoted the father's program as if it was a stable revenue source. For years, the agency's annual gala at the Waldorf Astoria was focused on the Children and Family Services Division, primarily because of the Head Start program; however, what was described as 'sexy' was the work I was doing with fathers.

I digress for a moment; however, imagine my surprise when I learned that VNS would hold its annual fundraiser at the infamous Waldorf Astoria, and that I and other members of the management team were invited to talk with potential donors about our program and the services we provided. It was a black-tie event, and we would be the guests of honor. I did not know it at the time; however, this would mark the beginning of a five-year annual event in which, on every occasion, more than a million dollars was raised for our division.

There was so much media attention around the fathers' program and our work towards the end of May and during the entire month of June, I was consumed, participating in interviews to discuss the program. I sat in front of cameras for more New York City news outlets than I can remember. I would have to say my favorite interview of all time was the interview Demetrius Ortiz and I did with Cindy Shue on Father's Day in 2010.

Jake McAfee was a documentary filmmaker working for former NBA all-star Allan Houston. He approached me with an interest in including the Bronx Fatherhood Program in a film he was making about fathers. Allan was a huge advocate for fathers and fathering programs. During his time playing for the New York Knicks, he held a faith-based camp upstate for children and their fathers that provided opportunities for fathers and sons to not only engage in sports activities but also workshops helping them to increase their knowledge and understanding of their role based upon biblical principles. I never had the opportunity to attend the camp; however, I understood it was well executed. I will not go into a long-drawn-out explanation of what happened; suffice it to say that the project never really got off the ground, and it was never discussed broadly because it would have been an embarrassing situation for Mr. Houston.

Coincidentally, a few months later, I was on a panel with Allan at Columbia University discussing the importance of fathers. We had dinner together, and for a world-renowned celebrity, I would have to say he was down-to-earth and extremely relatable. It was a pleasure to spend time getting to know him. The film project never came up.

So now I pick up where I left off with Ben. I introduced Ben to the group participants, explained why he was there, and began facilitating the group session. It was one of those days when the fathers, quite used to having guests and observers by now, were in rare form. It never mattered to them or me who was in the room; I always encouraged them to be themselves. It was important to me that anyone who came to observe the group saw them for who they were, not what was typically written about them.

They were engaged, sharing insightful stories, discussing challenges, and soliciting guidance from the group facilitators. Ben had never seen anything like it. The experience went totally against the grain of what was portrayed in the media and what he had researched as it relates to African American and Latino fathers. He shared with me that his father was deeply involved in all aspects of their care and upbringing. Ben and his brother, had a great relationship with their father. He was the beneficiary of many great hands-on parenting experiences, and, based on what he had observed, these 16 to 24-year-old non-custodial dads were no less committed. He also asked if it was ok for him to continue coming to our groups, and that eventually we would be in contact to see whether there was an angle he could present to the NY Times.

After a few months of attending groups, interviewing me, and following a couple of fathers around to gain insight into their lives and their stories, we had an eleven-minute film that surpassed our expectations. Ben initially planned to take photos and write a story as part of his pitch; however, once we saw how the story was coming together, I convinced him to make a short film. And he did, the editor loved the finished product.

The eleven-minute film, titled "Leon's Story," when it appeared in the *New York Times*, gained widespread attention. This resulted in Ben getting assigned more work, a lot of notoriety for the program, and several philanthropic organizations donated funds to the agency, earmarked for the Bronx Fatherhood program. I was delighted that we would be able to expand services because of the funding, and I was even more excited about the relationship I was developing with Ben.

So, confronted with this crazy desire to make a film, I reached out to Ben, and he immediately responded. One thing I have learned in the professional world is that you can gauge the depth of your relationship with someone by how long it takes for them to get back to you after you call. Not only did he respond quickly, but he actually seemed excited to talk with me. It had been a little over a year since we last communicated, and it was good to catch up. I shared my crazy idea with him and immediately launched into asking questions about the type of camera I should purchase and everything else I would need to do and learn about in order to make a film. I explained that by no means was I attempting to make light of his craft or profession; however, I believed that with his tutelage, I would be successful.

He reminded me that he was just a photographer who, with my encouragement, happened to make a successful film. I told him that he was more of a filmmaker than he knew himself to be. At some point, he asked me again what it was that I was attempting to do, what my motivation was, and what my anticipated outcome was. After listening to me and the rationale for my wanting to make the film, my desire to leave something meaningful to the field, he offered to shoot the film for me if I paid for the studio time and some of the editing costs. I agreed only if he allowed me to pay for his time as well. At the conclusion of that conversation, we had a verbal contract. It was now left up to me to conceptualize, write, and pull everything together.

This was another situation where I honestly had to trust what God was placing on my heart, and I just started with an outline and a list of tasks. I listed the support I would need from the fathers, who I thought would be willing and had compelling stories that would be impactful, based on their experiences and their resolve to overcome the challenges they'd faced to be actively involved fathers. I also wanted to support my eldest son and his craft. He graduated from college with a bachelor's in fine art, and this would be an opportunity to display his talent. Within a week, I had a solid outline, a theme, and a title for the documentary.

This was the language I wrote for the intro to the film: Fathering Me: The Long Walk Home; it is about the developmental trajectory many men must take in the absence of their biological fathers and/or any other positive male role model. It is about the collective successes and failures of young boys and men as they come to grips with the fact that a void needs to be filled.

Often, through corrective experiences and maturity, many of these men find their way fathering their offspring. While at the same time, they learn to heal their own wounds by fathering themselves. In the absence of their fathers, in most instances, their success is predicated on the notion that they grow up understanding the importance of family.

My next task was to organize the film's structure, select a few poems from my book Fathering Me: A Journey into Fatherhood that I felt would be impactful, and, lastly, think about the fathers I wanted to interview and how I would weave everything together.

I had to first decide on a good opening, how I would begin the story, and what would provide a good rationale for my selections.

Then I needed to decide what would be a good climax, how I would end the film. I decided that a powerful quote I came across would be a great way of opening the film.

"If you want to positively influence the life of a child, you have to begin about 100 years before he or she is born."

Oliver Wendell Holmes

I chose this quote because, to me, it spoke to the generational impact, the experiences that inform and influence what contributes to the healthy development of a child. It takes generations of healthy living and parenting success to not only learn but also convey that knowledge to your children in a way that positively impacts their development.

This is not a rehearsal; it is the real thing. I also needed to decide which poems or testimonies would enable me to adequately display the challenges fathers faced and how they overcame them or reconciled with their families. After thinking about the climax, I had to find a way to place a bow on the film, tying it together so there would be not only optimism but also hope. By some miracle, not only did it come together, but several questions arose that I believed would be important to answer. They came to me because I put myself in the audience to see if what I was proposing made sense. The questions were as follows:

Why this Documentary? Why Now? And how does this film tie into or connect with the work I've done to date? As I pondered this, one final question arose: what were our hopes and/or goals for the documentary? In other words, what did I expect practitioners to do?

Reflecting on the work I had done in the past and my experience in Memphis, I wanted to highlight fathers' capacity to make essential repairs and lift up the importance of their having corrective experiences with women. It is important for them to accept their circumstances, embrace failures, and intentionally educate themselves so they can engage and interact with their children in developmentally appropriate ways. It was important to emphasize the parallel process of their need to develop as men and fathers, while at the same time understanding the need to expand their role beyond financial providers. It was important for practitioners and staff engaging fathers to see what this would require of them. Emphasizing the generational impact of not having a positively engaged father and the time, energy, and effort it takes to become one was not going to be easy. And yet, I was able to successfully convey all the above.

Finally, helping fathers value and think of themselves as fathers first, which informs their decisions, was also going to be key. I had my videographer, and I was the director, producer, and writer. David Jr. would be the assistant director/producer and lead actor, and I finally settled on the fathers who would provide testimonials about their experiences in the program. I also had a supporting cast of other individuals connected to the program who would be included in the film. We were on our way!

Film Screenings and all that came after

- Private Screening in New York, Nomad Loft,
- James Madison University,
- Howard University,
- New York University,
- Paine College,
- Washington D.C., Mead Center Private Screening,
- James Madison,
- World Film Fair - Best Films Screening Producer's Club 10/27/2018
- World Film Fair Award Winner

Dear David,

We hope that you are well. We are contacting you today to inform you that we have been invited by the World Film Fair, a large-scale film market event, to take part in their Fair, which will be held in New York in October 2018. More information about the World Film Fair can be found on their website: https://worldfilmfair.com/

This is a very exciting opportunity for our festival and our filmmakers as it means the films, which make it to the official selection stage of our festival, will now be shown on a larger platform to not only an international audience of film goers but also to a arrange of distributors, production companies, and film investors. You will, of course, be welcome to attend the Fair as part of our festival and take advantage of the opportunity to network with the other filmmakers and industry professionals that will be in attendance.

Therefore, we have made the decision to amend the date of the 2018 edition of the festival and to hold it exclusively at the World Film Fair. We apologize if this causes any inconvenience, but we are confident that hosting our festival at the World Film Fair will be very beneficial for the films submitted to our festival and is too good of an opportunity to miss out on.

If you have questions or require any further information, please let us know,

Best Regards,

Washington Film Festival Support Team

FATHERING ME: THE LONG WALK HOME

Getting to the Heart
(Strategies & Training)

"I can't think of any need in a child's life as strong as the need for a father's love and protection."

What does it take, really? In my estimation, it's someone, anyone, who sees going the extra mile as the norm! Professionals with the ability to manage their frustrations and, despite their instincts, continue to provide guidance and support for individuals who, at times, will do everything in their power to demonstrate that is the last thing they want. It means operating with a sense of clarity even in the fog and hoping for the best. What may seem impossible to some people can be achieved with the right support. As practitioners, what are our goals when it comes to engaging fathers?

What is the rationale, and why do we do what we do?

This book will help you:

- E nhance your capacity to think and reflect upon your current knowledge and how it can be a springboard to help you build upon that knowledge.

- Explore the rationale for engaging fathers within your respective place.

- Evaluate the fathers' role in the family and how impending fatherhood/parenthood affects men and how they respond to the fathering experience.

- Evaluate the fathers' role in the family and how impending fatherhood/parenthood affects men and how they respond to the fathering experience.

- Expand your understanding of the many role's fathers play and the importance of redefining those roles.

- Help you gain strategies and skills supporting father engagement in all aspects of service delivery.

Why Focus on Fathers? We are all aware, or should be, of the data as professionals dedicating our energy and efforts to this work. Children from fatherless homes are:

- Less likely to attend college.

- More likely to be incarcerated

- More likely to have children out of wedlock

- Less likely to marry

- More likely to divorce if they marry

- Children from single-mother households earn less as adults than children from two parent families, and

- Children from single-mother households are more likely to be poor as adults and use government services.

According to the Research

- "Early father involvement predicts continued involvement.

- "Men are fully capable of nurturing young children.

- "Fathers become attached to their infants."

I reference this research because it influenced my early thinking about how best to serve fathers. This is my way of paying homage, and although their research was not focused on African American and Latino males, it was applicable. I have been committed to this work for almost 30 years, and while current thinking has expanded on what these pioneers stated, these statements hold true today.

I think most of you, as individuals engaged in the work, would agree with this quote, "The course of development can be altered in early childhood by effective interventions that change the balance between risk and protection, thereby shifting the odds in favor of more adaptive outcomes."
Jack Shonkoff, Neurons to Neighborhoods.

Which reminds us of our charge: to help practitioners focus on what is in our children's best interest. The things we can do to help them recover from adverse childhood experiences, and how to ensure fathers are knowledgeable enough to prevent those same experiences from occurring in their children's lives.

The Notion of Gifts

"A man who trims himself to suit everybody will
soon whittle himself away."

(C. Schwab)

What important gifts did you receive from your father? Traveling all over the country, this tends to be one of the most interesting questions I ask a group of training attendees. Of all the years that I spent in the business, there is one phenomenon that still baffles me when I spend time with professionals who say they are interested in enhancing their capacity to engage fathers, and yet when I walk into the room or training facility, there is a tension that is so thick that you can cut it with a knife, especially when they know in advance that the topic is father engagement. To be honest, there were groups I engaged in planning their content around their needs, based on the questions they were seeking answers to, and they still struggled when the training began.

They asked, Will I address a particular aspect of the work? Am I able to? Or are we going to discuss domestic violence, fathers who are abusers, etc.? These questions speak to their inherent fears or to some of the challenging aspects of the work they have attempted to deal with in the past or, in some instances, avoided. There are other situations where I do not expect it to be, and yet the experiences are quite similar.

I have trained at the national, state, and local levels across the East Coast, from New York and Puerto Rico to Hawaii. In 2007, I was the opening Keynote Speaker at the World Forum on Men in Early Childhood Education in Hawaii, where fathers and men seeking to engage men in the early childhood field from all over the world came together to learn and share their approaches to the work. Topics addressed included the historical context of men in early childhood, research on men in early childhood, myths and stereotypes about men in early childhood, constraints on achieving gender balance, success stories, and proven strategies for improving gender balance.

I was part of a three-presenter plenary discussion with Kekoa Harman, a Teacher from Aha Punana Leo, Inc., Hawaii; Tymothy Smith, a Consultant, Early Care and Education, Texas; and me, the Division Director of Family Support Services at Visiting Nurse Service of New York. It was an honor to participate in an event that brought together seasoned professionals from around the world (Africa, Australia, the Netherlands, Belgium, Scotland, and the United States).

I spoke about staff's ability to self-assess, analyze, and reflect openly and honestly on their past experiences with men. I emphasized how important it is for them to understand that their inability to self-assess can affect their ability to engage with parents respectfully.

Finally, given the influx of women in the workforce at the time, fathers are increasingly engaged as full partners in caring for their children, and practitioners need to be responsive to this change.

Whether it is an opening keynote, an individual session, or a panel, this has been one of the most difficult questions I have ever asked a group of training attendees. Suffice it to say that talking about fathers is a trigger for some staff and practitioners. The thing I have learned is that the responses I receive are contingent on a few factors, including whether the relationship with one's father was good, not so good, or complex.

Was he absent, present, or presently absent? Was he gentle, kind, authoritarian, a dictator, an effective communicator, an abuser, someone who listened to your needs, or was he strict, and the conversations were often one-sided? I am hoping that you get my point! These factors cause one not only to reflect on their own personal experience but also to reflect on expectations in their personal lives as well as in a professional setting, which shapes the expectations they create for fathers. Once attendees can reconcile and respond to the first part of the question, they then move on.

Did he give the gift of time? The gift of understanding the importance of obtaining a good education? What about survival skills or the gift of a love of sports and an understanding of the need to invest in athletic training?

Were these experiences positive or not so much? Was he attempting to vicariously relive his successes or failures through his children? How did or does this shape your expectations of what a father should be doing? What impact has it had on you as an individual?

After gaining insight into how difficult these conversations could be, my decision to use poetry to desensitize the experience for attendees was instrumental in facilitating this conversation as well. Using poetry as an icebreaker was ingenious and proved to be an important shift in my facilitation approach.

Perceptions of Fathers

I would be remiss if I did not discuss the negative attitudes about a father's role. It pains me to admit this; however, fathers sometimes are their own worst enemies because they buy into other people's perceptions or beliefs about their role and what their fathering practices should look like.

- Still to this day in 2025, dads are viewed as "the other parent" by moms and family members.

- The societal prescribed definition of men being viewed as financial providers is so limiting because it does not provide opportunities for men to see themselves in other roles that are significant for their child's and their own development.

- Society often assumes that men do not want to be actively engaged in their children's lives, which is not true.

- Fathers sometimes buy into the notion, minimizing their role by viewing themselves as "part-time assistants" to the mom.

While it is true in many instances fathers are not the custodial parent, nor are they frequently engaged in specific aspects of child rearing practices, it does not mean they are incapable of doing it.

Positioning oneself as "the other parent" aligns \ `` lot of the problematic thinking embedded in man of our systems designed to support children and families. They think of mothers first and only if they cannot contact and communicate with the mother, they reluctantly reach out to the father.

I have mentioned a few times; however, it is worth mentioning again that fathers must expand their definition of their role, so that they embrace, subscribe to, and engage in all aspects of parenting that go well beyond just being a financial provider. This will help establish a culture in which they are viewed holistically for everything they can bring to the parenting table.

Men are not only willing to engage, but they want to engage. Many of them have not been shown the way, so they are not only hesitant but also fearful. They do not want it known that they do not know what to do. That they are afraid they might injure their child or do something worse. Working with professionals who establish trusting relationships with fathers enables them to open up and disclose their concerns, fears, and challenges as they embrace the role.

Barriers to Involvement/Engagement

What are some of the distinct and unique barriers to father involvement, and how are they different from father engagement? I couch them in two buckets: personal life barriers that affect the decision to be involved and the ability to do so. Then we must evaluate and understand their response to programmatic expectations and perceived demands.

Barriers to Involvement:

- Not having adequate childcare.

- Difficulty transitioning into the fathering/parenting role.

- The impact of inclement weather and how it informs the decisions some parents make regarding venturing out of their homes.

- Work obligations that prevent fathers from engaging in programmatic activities when service delivery is not responsive to alternative schedules.

- Limited transportation options, especially when families reside outside urban areas.

- Scheduling conflicts in general limit access to service delivery.

Barriers to Engagement:

- Rigid and inflexible programmatic expectations.

- Inherent fear and distrust of the systems they must navigate to receive services.

- Feelings of being unwelcome and disrespected by professionals who are supposed to help.

- This is usually based on inconsistent recruitment efforts by the program.

- Fathers are misunderstood, and programs do not do enough to help them learn how their past informs their present and future behavior.

- There is an inherent power imbalance between fathers and the individuals they must encounter, who can make decisions that could alter the course of their lives.

- Role misalignment between fathers and individuals in the helping professions, who are anchored in unrealistic expectations.

- Inability to establish trust.

Then there are a few additional barriers, challenges that many men face but are particularly unique to younger fathers.

- They do not have enough money to contribute financially in a meaningful way and lack the essential resources needed to fulfill their responsibilities as fathers.

- In many instances, they have not completed their formal education, i.e., they did not obtain a high school diploma or a general equivalent degree.

- There is an inherent lack of knowledge and preparedness for the role, as they are void of positive role models.

- There are emotional, social, and sexual changes that occur for men that affect their relationship with their partner. If these changes are not recognized, they may lead to stress and impairment in their psychological functioning.

- This is even more complicated if we are dealing with men who are already in compromising mental health situations.

- They have not learned the essential tenets of effective communication, and face challenges conversing with their child's mother, maternal and paternal grandparents, and professionals working within the systems they must navigate to gain access to their child.

- There is limited father-specific programming in their communities to help them develop the necessary skills they need to learn, grow, and succeed.

- Many are still struggling with adolescent development and are in a parallel process of development with their child.

- Poverty is defined as being poor. What is not often acknowledged is that experiencing poverty creates desperation in some individuals, where they are willing to do anything and everything to try and change their immediate circumstances, often to their own detriment.

- It is also important to understand the feminized culture of childcare, early childhood education settings, the health care system, and social services. All of which are not as responsive to men as they are to women.

———————⌒⌒———————

The Elephant

"The father of the righteous will greatly rejoice; he who fathers a wise son will be glad in him."
Proverbs 23:24

Of course, we would be remiss if we did not talk about the final and in many instances the most significant barrier, which I refer to as the elephant in the room. It is important to note that acknowledging this truth can evoke fear and challenge practitioners' sense of safety when working with fathers in need of assistance.

I recently had a discussion where, as I typically do, I tried to delicately discuss a controversial topic with care and consideration, grounded in a truth that some people do not like to acknowledge or accept. Usually, at the beginning and end of my trainings, I discuss the importance of feedback from evaluation surveys, whether they are my own or surveys disseminated by the host. I value feedback, as it is a way for me to assess whether the content was appropriate, whether I did a decent job delivering the material and conveying the most salient points, and it provides me an opportunity to obtain real time feedback so that I can course correct, enhance, and improve in areas that did not work.

"When I received the feedback survey one participant shared, I felt uncomfortable with the presenter giving information that he stated others might consider dated albeit foundational. Additionally, when he addressed domestic violence and used the term "beating" on a woman it did not feel good to me. I am a survivor of domestic violence. His statement that women also commit domestic violence against men felt like minimization of what women globally experience at the hands of male violence. As a woman, I happen to have experienced domestic violence from a female partner, so I am aware that anyone can be an abuser. I found the flippant way with which he discussed and brought up domestic violence unsettling." Anonymous Feedback

Ninety-eight percent of the feedback I received was exceptional, and yet, I could not get over the fact that this individual was deeply offended by the domestic violence portion of the discussion.

Negating the fact that she had totally misconstrued my comments and my intent. I reflected, thinking that if I had the opportunity to talk with the individual, I would have taken great care to help her understand that I was drawing upon and speaking about data I collected. My comments were not my opinion. I spoke of the knowledge and experience I gained working with men who battered and those who were battered. I would never minimize the effects of an issue as serious as domestic violence. It was also apparent, through no fault of my own, that when individuals have not dealt with their own past trauma, discussions like these can be a potential trigger.

At any rate, the fact remains that:

"Violence and thinking are mutually exclusive. Thinking reflects the capacity to represent mental content in symbolic form. This mental conflict can be articulated and described to others, which brings a sense of relief. Violence, on the other hand, signifies the breakdown of thought and the failure of words, but it is powerful communication nonetheless, one which can have devastating consequences. Violence is communication at such a primitive level that it bypasses thought altogether, and consequently the dialogue between the victim, the perpetrator and society occurs at a level that is beyond awareness." *S. Blumenthal*

• Men sometimes behave badly, and this colors the complexion of how they are viewed and whether practitioners choose to engage them

• There are instances where they have abandoned their children

• Sometimes they are authoritarian

• In other instances, they are strong disciplinarians, embracing physical abuse as a method of correction

• Sometimes they are perpetrators of domestic violence

• They sometimes use and abuse substances

So, what is our charge when we engage a father facing one or more of these challenges? It is our responsibility to assist by providing or connecting them with resources that will help them learn the importance of being intentionally different. They may not fully understand how their behavior is affecting their child, children, and/or family.

In the case of domestic violence, we would be remiss if we walked away from a father once we discovered that he has serious communication and self-regulation issues. In case you were not aware or never thought of it in this manner, violence, hitting, is a form of communication, one that an individual resorts to when they either fail to or, in the moment, are incapable of using their words.

I experienced many situations, when I was a director, where I was judged harshly by female staff who aligned with a mother who was a victim of domestic violence, because I asked insightful questions about the circumstances surrounding the violence. In their minds, I was looking for justification or seeking to validate why the father resorted to using violence as a form of communication.

My only goal in asking those questions was to ascertain whether this individual might be someone we could work with and get him the support, i.e., counseling and or long-term intense therapy, he needed to change his behavior. My rationale is simple: most often, these individuals are not only charismatic but also controlling, and if we allow them to walk away from these situations without taking any responsibility, they will find someone else to batter! It is also important to recognize that:

It is unfortunate that many practitioners see a deficit model when looking at fathers, which makes sense to some degree because it is how they qualify for services; however, I have always tried to look at potential strengths. This helped me adopt a more optimistic lens toward the possibilities.

Once a relationship had been formed and we were on our way to building trust, I could leverage those strengths to help them begin to address challenges and obstacles preventing them from achieving their goals. Given what we know now, it is important to ensure that practitioners receive the necessary professional development. They will require training that provides them with a depth of understanding of the issues that fathers have experienced in their past. This requires tremendous flexibility in their acceptance of fathers when they meet them and begin to explore expectations regarding what they can do.

This is an opportune time to share a story of how I helped several staff members, but one staff member in particular, transition from minimizing the significance, role, and contributions of fathers to being the program's greatest advocate and champion for fathers. It took a great deal of introspective thought and self-reflection, as well as intentional behavior modification, to develop the capacity to initially see the fathers, then to appreciate what they were bringing to the table, and finally to appropriately engage them in meaningful conversations about their child/family.

Why should it be any different for fathers? (Professional Development Impact)

"Children, obey your parents in the Lord, for this is right."
Ephesians 6:1

A female staff person from a Head Start Program reflects on how she improved her ability to engage fathers. This would not have been possible if we as an organization hadn't begun investing in scaffolding our knowledge of what father engagement really entailed. We invested in the requisite professional development, individual supervision, held conversations, was able to identify challenges some of the staff were experiencing, and we intentionally had more discussions with staff during reflective supervision.

"To me, fathers were always looked at as secondary caregivers. In my eyes, they were good enough to drop off and pick up their children and attend a parent/teacher conference or two, but for serious matters, I thought it was best to speak with the children's mothers, grandmothers, or aunts. It was not until these issues were addressed and discussed during weekly staff developments that my outlook on fatherhood began to change. The staff developments focused on the meaning of fatherhood and the important roles that fathers play in the lives of their children. I had to not only pay attention to the positive interactions that the fathers in the program had with their children, but also to my own interactions with the father when they came into the center.

I became more self-aware and realized that I was rarely welcoming or engaging with the fathers and gave them the sense that they did not truly belong in the center. The training and meaningful discussions that I had with my colleagues changed how I saw fathers and their children. It gave me a safe environment to tap into deep emotions that caused me to disregard fathers, and I was taught how to overcome the results of negative past experiences with men so that I could move forward in a healthy way, serving both the mothers and fathers in the program."

HS Head Teacher

This is an amazing real-life example of what can happen when an organization embraces a true commitment and investment in professional development. The professional development cannot and must not be a one off. It must be well thought out, planned and executed overtime as an essential consideration and component of service delivery where all staff are held accountable, and they embrace the notion that father engagement is everybody's business. If done the right way, it can contribute to meaningful change for staff, which, in this instance, resulted in enhanced communication, engagement, and interactions with fathers.

What is also interesting about this story is that these were fathers that were 'somewhat involved,' they were trying, they were showing up to pick up their children, and they were willing to engage with educators. The challenge, at least in this situation, based upon the lens of this employee, the fathers were not recipients of respectful service delivery. It is essential that agencies, programs, and organizations that serve families conduct an environmental scan periodically to assess how they are doing with father engagement to ensure that they are thoughtful and intentional and that fathers are having a meaningful experience when they walk through the doors.

D. Jones Program Director

Building Curiosity
By the way, it didn't kill the cat!

How can we help organizations make this critical shift? It is imperative that organizations find ways to be intentionally different by doing the things outlined below. The question, of course, is how? Are you curious about fathers and what abilities they might have that would contribute to their success? The pivotal shift begins with the inherent belief that fathers are important to their children, families, and communities.

- Focus on building meaningful relationships with fathers. Conversations that are grounded in genuine curiosity are a great way to begin. And while some fathers might be a little hesitant at first, stay the course, and eventually they will open up and begin not only to respond but also to share what is important to them with respect to their role as fathers.

- Assess, evaluate, and explore program leadership, continuous improvement, and staff professional development to enhance father engagement. These strategies can help ensure your program is committed to fostering a culture of inclusion. It is not enough to review your progress towards creating an environment that is welcoming to fathers; leadership's support is crucial, whether through amending and/or drafting policies and procedures, supporting the work, or securing fiscal support to drive initiatives.

- Evaluating and tweaking efforts is important for growth. Meeting with staff to discuss their on-going challenges and successes is equally important.

- Help staff learn to assess a father's interest and goals for his child/family. A father's focus on his child is not always visually apparent. There are cognitive processes taking place all the time, in which they hold their children in mind, hoping they are learning, growing, and benefiting from our efforts. Having an exploratory verbal with fathers can result in our helping them refine their goals and actively pursue them with our guidance and support.

- Hold "real" conversations with fathers. This might sometimes involve difficult conversations about behavior and attitude adjustments. It is important to remember that these are men who have had years of individuals telling them what to do and how to do it. Helping fathers recognize how to use their inherent skills and overcome obstacles is vital. Educating them whenever possible about the importance of cognitive processes and how their thoughts connect to decision-making is key. What is important here is congruence between what they are saying and what they are doing. Plan targeted interventions based upon those newly discovered interests and goals.

- Explore the father's goals for his own developmental trajectory as well, to place him in a better position to achieve more work-life balance, if possible.

- Our outcomes for fathers are better when the solutions are tailored to a father's specific needs. There is no quick fix!

- Shifting gender expectations can leave some parents feeling confused, hurt, and angry. It can result in clashes between men and women opposed to sharing parenting roles/practices. Also, there are distinct disadvantages for some women when fathers are knowledgeable advocates for themselves and their children.

> "A genuine desire to engage and connect can get lost in an environment that suggest otherwise. Everyone remotely involved in programs interested in supporting fathers/men can be instrumental in Creating a Culture of Inclusion." David A. Jones, Sr.

We have talked a great deal about what is necessary to move from involvement to meaningful and sustained engagement. We talked about some research, the barriers, and the need for staff professional development.

Now it is time to talk about the benefits and some of the outcomes one might expect to see after the time invested in Creating a Culture of Inclusion.

Bringing it Home
The Bronx Fatherhood Program

Success is the maximum utilization of the ability
that you have.

The 'Bronx Fatherhood Program,' was the culmination of efforts that began in Far Rockaway, Queens, in 1995. This was an opportunity to crystallize all the great work I deemed to be the litmus test for designing and delivering quality services to a population that mainstream media suggested was not interested in their children or fathering practices. After several years of success and a slight step away from direct service to regroup, my organization worked with me to respond to a Request for Proposal with the Department of Youth and Community Development.

We were awarded funding to provide full-service programming for 16 to 24-year-old non-custodial fathers. I was ecstatic at the thought of having the opportunity to provide full-service programming for fathers.

What would that even look like? I had some elements of the structure and a strong foundation; however, I would have to evaluate and consider what additional services would be needed and how I would do what was necessary with limited staff. It would be me as the Director, a Project Coordinator, and two Outreach Workers as the full-time staff. Founded in 2007, my initial focus was on program start-up and service design based on what had been successfully implemented in the Fathers First program.

Service delivery began in February 2008. That was also the day I began training my successors. I said to them, Today is a pivotal day in the life of the program, and in some respects, it is bittersweet. I have to find a way to pass on my knowledge and philosophical approach to this work and do it well enough to instill confidence in each of you to be able to do this work and hopefully improve upon what has already been created.

This, for me, was also monumental and instrumental at the same time. It was a homecoming for me to return to the neighborhood where I grew up and lived as a child, and to bring meaningful services to a community that really needed them. Yes, my team and I would be responsible for providing concrete services to young fathers residing in the South Bronx. It was unreal.

Program Structure - Impacts

It is important to discuss and develop specific, measurable programmatic impacts that contribute to meaningful outcomes possible as a result of the aforementioned investments. Listed below are examples of what I was able to do with both programs. One that was initially focused on supporting adolescent parents enrolled in the Early Head Start program in Far Rockaway, Queens, NY. And the other is a full-service, 5 day a week one stop shop program designed specifically for 16 to 24-year-old non-custodial fathers, in the "Boogie Down," aka the Bronx.

This was an opportunity to provide comprehensive services. Our efforts to recruit, enroll, engage, and service these men far exceeded our expectations. And I must admit, it is rare that we, as practitioners, get to experience this type of behavior modification in the families we meet and serve throughout our lifetime. Our success was grounded in our attitudes towards these men and the inherent belief in their potential. We engaged them in activities while providing the structure they needed to succeed.

Things like assistance with planning, goal setting, and following through. All of which is no different from what we have been doing with and for mothers for years. Drawing upon my clinical training, I followed a principle that works extremely well with young children. Once I understood the fathers, a little about their past and their immediate needs, we partnered on goal setting, and I followed their lead, working with them at their pace, refining their goals as necessary, given their unique circumstances.

You see, if you really want to meet with success supporting fathers, try not to be so prescriptive. And I have to say it took years before I could genuinely appreciate the magnitude of what we were able to accomplish, and for that, I know we were truly blessed. These accomplishments were only possible because we were fortunate enough to have the following structural components in place.

• Organizations, to the extent possible, need to provide comprehensive services. It is understandable that, within your respective space, you might not be able to provide an array of services for fathers; however, referrals to community resources and partner agencies can be meaningful in helping them achieve a particular goal. In addition, your time with the father might be very targeted, and based upon a finite amount of time, try as best you can to make the time not only memorable for you and the father but also beneficial in helping him gain insight or new knowledge that he can utilize in the present and potentially in the future.

• Whenever possible, seek additional funding and foundation support. Solid funding can be obtained by maximizing opportunities to have multiple funding streams, collecting data on your impacts and outcomes, and telling your story. Additional funding enables organizations to provide clients with resources and incentives to support successful engagement. Something as simple as a transportation gift card or books they can read to their children is ideal.

• Solid, well-trained staff who are willing to continue enhancing their skills contribute to the development of competent, independent practitioners. It also helps to build that culture of inclusion, which should be the goal for all programs.

• Provide quality supervision and on-going professional development for staff. It is important to have dedicated time with a supervisor to review and process intervention attempts. We will not always get it right the first time; however, being able to bounce ideas off an experienced supervisor who can not only support you but also guide and encourage you to continue taking calculated risks is essential.

If our hearts and minds are in the right place and we are thoughtful and intentional in our efforts to connect and build meaningful relationships with fathers, it is rare that we will make a mistake from which we cannot recover.

• It is essential to have staff in a leadership role with clinical expertise. When asked about my skills and unique ability to achieve success in engaging fathers, I attribute it to my passion, authenticity, commitment, persistence, and clinical expertise. My ability to fully understand a person in their unique situation and to skillfully align with them, while assessing their intrinsic and extrinsic motivations for doing what they do and, in some cases, helping them discover what those motivations were, paid great dividends. Helping individuals recognize how to use their inherent skills to overcome obstacles, and educating them whenever possible about the importance of cognitive processes and how their thoughts connect to decision-making, is also valuable. It is important to emphasize that there is no one right way to parent, and there is no such thing as a perfect parent. We are all learning the essential skills for good enough parenting as we go along. What is clear is that there are some definite things parents should try to avoid, and that is a place for meaningful discussion and perhaps common understanding.

Program Outcomes

Increased parenting competency and communication skills

It is a well-known fact that society does not prepare men for the parenting experience in the same way it prepares mothers. From the time a woman becomes pregnant, if she is engaged in prenatal care, her knowledge is constantly scaffolded by the systems she must navigate in an effort to bring forth a healthy child. During her prenatal appointments, she learns about the developing fetus, her diet and nutrition, and how to ensure she is taking proper care of herself in preparation for the delivery. She is asked questions about her beliefs and preferences, and she is referred to WIC, where she receives additional nutrition information for herself and the baby, as well as for other members of her family. In some instances, there are inquiries about the father and whether he is involved. If there is a healthy relationship and he is available, he might receive some of the same information. If he is fortunate to be connected to a program that offers services for fathers and provides educational workshops, he might receive similar information. This inherently places the father at a disadvantage in enhancing his capacity to respond to fathering tasks. Recognizing this fact, we were thoughtful and intentional about providing fathers with a depth of understanding of some of the foundational information needed to attune and attend to their partners' needs if they were in a relationship, and if not, essential aspects of newborn care when and if they had the opportunity to engage with their child.

From basic techniques, like how to feed and hold his child and not be afraid. The importance of talking softly to the child, maintaining eye and skin-to-skin contact, and a few other things. We discussed post-partum depression, the signs and symptoms, and how important it would be for him to be a support for mom and baby if they faced this situation. In some instances, the ways in which many of these fathers learned to communicate were not healthy. If the father experienced gatekeeping preventing his access to the child or if the family were involved with institutions making decisions about his access, we would explain how important it was for him to remain calm, ask specific questions, and follow through with all directives to meet those expectations. Individual sessions, or during groups, were the appropriate places to vent frustrations. These strategies contributed to their success in a few situations, and they learned to model appropriate behavior for their children.

Prenatal Experience

Thoughts about working with expectant men influenced by a grounded theory study of men during their partner's pregnancies. A large number of fathers are ambivalent, reluctant, and concerned about how to define their new role. They are concerned about embracing a new life and wrestling with thoughts about sustaining the relationship with their partner. This is a time and place for candid conversations amongst couples and professionals supporting them. Most antenatal classes do not meet the needs of male partners who are prepared and, in some respects, ready to accept the baby and increased responsibility. What about men who are grounded in a place of struggle, with themselves, their relationship, and are conflicted about parenting. The chart below illustrates what may happen when parents learn they are having a baby. They may begin at a similar place, disbelief and shock, and then move through various stages of acceptance and denial, finally dealing with the reality of their newborn.

There are usually a few instances when parents may share similar feelings at the same time. Much of which is contingent on the strength of their relationship and their ability to communicate effectively throughout the stages, which may affect how they cope with parenting.

Female experience	Male experience
Psychological	Psychological
Physiological	Vicarious
Ambivalence, excitement, fear	Ambivalence, fear, concern
Acceptance	Acceptance, indifference, refusal
Primary roles	Participation not guaranteed (may be optional)
Prenatal visits	Participation not guaranteed (may be optional)
Sonogram (excitement anticipation)	Sonogram (pregnancy becomes real
Intimate relationship with child, attachment, and bonding	Supportive relationship with child (contingent on relationship with mother)

- Fathers sometimes require support to embrace their parenting responsibilities

- Explore the nature of the relationship between expectant parents. Discuss specific supports that may be needed/helpful

- When evaluating how to work with expectant fathers to help them understand their role and responsibilities, consider the level of acceptance, readiness, and preparation. Did they want to have a child?

- What do we consider to be appropriate supports for expectant fathers?

Just for fun: Terminology we use in many ECE and parenting programs.

- ASQ & Denver Assessments

- Cognitive

- Doula

- Development

- Episiotomy

- Fine Motor

- Gestation

- Gross Motor

- Lactation

- Placenta

- Social & Emotional

- Trimester

- Uterus

Thomas Walkers' Story

Thomas Walker was the first mandated client I ever enrolled in the Fathers First program. He was referred for individual counseling by the Bronx Family Court. During our first session, it was clear that he was reluctant to meet with me. It was not personal, but after our conversation began, it was apparent; he did not think he should have to meet with me, he was not happy with the referral, and he honestly felt, with every fiber of his being, that it was his wife who had the problem.

After a few sessions, I found Thomas to be a good man, a man with integrity, a hard worker, a man devoted to martial arts and his family. The only problem was he had narrowly defined his role. In fact, he totally and completely subscribed to the societal definition of what a father should be, which was a financial provider. He was a cab driver, who worked long hours to provide for his family. All the household duties, including taking care of his children, their educational pursuits, were his wife's responsibility.

I won't go into detail; however, under the wife's supervision, it was disclosed that some inappropriate things were taking place in the presence of the children that involved controlled substances, and they were removed from the family and placed in the system. Thomas went to court and told the judge that he had nothing to do with what happened, that he was at work, and that the judge needed to return his children to him forthwith. The children were placed in foster care, and he was mandated to get counseling and parenting skills training.

What Thomas failed to understand was that he and his wife were equally responsible for their children's welfare. When he learned more about what was actually taking place in the home, he was stunned. Not only were the children placed in a situation where they witnessed inappropriate adult behavior, but his daughter had also missed a significant number of days from school. He was not aware, did not have a clue. If this were a wrestling match, it was time for him to tap in, and if his team were to win, he would need a serious takedown and a pin.

My support for Thomas centered on enhancing his understanding of his role and responsibilities. We discussed specific tasks not rooted in gender prescribed roles. We discussed how this benefited not only the children but the entire family. After a few individual sessions with me, I invited him to come to the fathers' groups with some of the younger dads. That is where he received additional insight into an expanded definition of the father's role. I began to see a flicker, a steady blink, and 'Viola," the light came on. Six months later, he was a different man when he went back to court. Unlike his first court appearance, where he jumped out of his taxi and showed up in casual clothing, he was informed; he was well-groomed and had on a suit and tie. Humbled by the experience, this is the letter he wrote and read to the judge.

T. Walker's Letter

"Your Honor,

I would like to take this time to thank you for taking this opportunity to hear about my case.

I would like to begin by saying I am extremely nervous. This is the hardest thing I have ever had to do. When I was here the last time, I was incorrect in thinking that because I was my children's biological parent that custody would automatically be granted to me. I did not even respond initially to the conditions mandated by this court, which would enable me to get my children back. When I discovered my son was being considered for adoption, reality set in. I know in some ways I have neglected my children in the past. I was emotionally spent by the break-up of my marriage and my family, so I ran. I have since worked hard to meet the conditions of the court by attending parenting classes, obtaining a larger apartment, undergoing drug screenings, and ensuring consistent visitation. What I have learned is mind boggling in that I realize there is so much more to being a parent than I was aware of. The parenting classes have opened my eyes to the fact that I have to be available and ready to respond to all of my children's needs. I love my children. I know I don't have the answer to all the problems and challenges they will face, yet I know I will make myself available. I will show them love and seek any necessary help to ensure their needs are met. I want to build special relationships with my children. I only hope that after today, you will see fit to give me the chance."

I could not provide a better example of increased parenting competency, which is why I thought this would be an ideal place for his story!

Increased number and quantity of positive parent-child (father-child) interactions:

Once the fathers were educated about their children's development and the things they could do to support that development, their confidence and competence improved. They were able to meet their children's needs, calming, nurturing, soothing, and caring for them in developmentally appropriate ways. These interactions strengthened the bond between the fathers and their children. Now they were ready to fully commit their time and the limited resources, often neglecting their own needs to ensure their children had the essentials. The education we provided about their cognitive development and how fathers can inform and influence their children's brain development was appealing to many of the fathers.

Improved parent communication and co-parenting relationships:

We discussed the need for fathers to improve their ability to communicate. It was important for them to regulate their behavior when conversing with the other parent, especially after the romantic relationship ended. Managing frustrations related to unrealistic expectations, or when mothers chose to gatekeep and prevent their involvement, were scenarios we discussed to help them learn how to successfully navigate these situations when they arose. Before continuing, it is important to address the notion of gatekeeping, which essentially is the activity of controlling and usually limiting general access to something, which is not always a bad thing, especially in situations where a father has had difficulty demonstrating appropriate behavior during their interactions with the child. The most important takeaway here was to keep the focus on what was in the child's best interest and to be patient, recognizing that the most important change might not happen overnight.

This is where educating fathers about their legal rights was information they needed to understand. So, if the other parent refused to cooperate, i.e., gatekeeping, they would have options. Community Partnerships can also be important here. In Queens, I established a partnership with LIFT, an organization that provided Pro Bono legal support specifically for fathers, helping them understand and advocate for their rights in Family Court.

Increased self-initiated child support payments:

When fathers are in a healthy co-parenting relationship and they have a steady income, financially contributing to their child's well-being is usually not an issue. Educating fathers about how beneficial it is for children to have engaged fathers who support them financially helped fathers see how important their support could be. In some instances, fathers become overly concerned with what the mother is doing with the resources he is providing, especially if, in his observations, he sees that his child's basic needs are not being met. Helping fathers understand that co-parenting requires both individuals to cooperate and be patient is a strategy we use to help them navigate difficult situations. Setting clear expectations and developing a parenting plan is necessary to shift the focus back to where it should be: the child's needs. Establishing formal payments through the courts increases the likelihood that children receive what has been allotted, and it avoids payment arrears.

Increased educational, vocational, and workforce participation:

The way society defines the father's role contributes to unrealistic expectations for many fathers. Coming from marginalized communities where they are still attempting to address their own needs, after having faced challenges navigating institutions that are supposed to prepare them to be contributing members of society, they are behind. Now saddled with the awesome responsibility of caring for and providing for another human being, they begin to take life more seriously. They are open to setting goals, planning, and getting a high school diploma, if they have not already done so. They are open to exploring other vocational opportunities, such as trades, that will give them the skills to earn a decent income so they can provide for their child and take care of themselves. Because society does not willingly give these men opportunities, programs must be able to create pathways for them to invest in themselves so that they can invest in their children and, at some point, in the viability and sustainability of their communities.

Here is an opportunity to explore their past, help them continue to focus on the good decisions they have made, rethink some of the not-so-good decisions, and begin to envision a plan for their future that helps them launch. Challenging fathers to understand their circumstances and to think differently about their capacity to change those circumstances is the way in which we get them to not only see the importance of investing in themselves but also ensure that they are preventing their children from having a similar experience. This is where we explore fathers' understanding of the ecosystem within which they live and how it informs and influences everything that is taking place.

Behavior modification is evidenced by decreases in the following areas:

In most cases of child abuse and neglect, parents repeat the behaviors they experienced as children. It is a known fact that the abused have a greater propensity to abuse if they were physically punished or beaten by their parents, unless they are educated about how damaging physical punishment can be and how it perpetuates a negative cycle. Once fathers are educated about the true meaning of discipline, which is to teach, they tend to almost immediately attempt to modify their behavior, asking for other developmentally appropriate practices to draw upon when responding to their child's challenging behaviors. Fathers who are healthy and in their right mind do not choose to harm their child. Having conversations with them about how their past experiences of being parented, good, bad, or indifferent, spill over into their parenting practices pays dividends in helping them readjust and realign their thinking.

Substance use and abuse: It helps to educate fathers about substance use and abuse and how it connects to something in their past or present that they are not able to deal with in a healthy way. It also compromises their ability to respond appropriately to their children's needs. Children are at risk when parents are under the influence of substances, and there are serious repercussions for parents if something happens to a child when they are in their care if they are using drugs. Again, helping fathers drill down and get to the source of their problem. Understanding what they are masking or defending against is helpful in providing them with the requisite information and insight they need, enabling them to invest in necessary change, even if it means going into a rehabilitation program.

Some of these men were abused by their parents, some were abandoned, some were in foster care, others will tell you they were never parented in a healthy way, so they are ill-equipped when it comes to fulfilling the role. The strategy here is to provide them with the necessary insight, education, and referrals, as appropriate, to address their issues.

Court involvement: Helping fathers understand that subscribing to the societal prescribed definition of the father's role when they have not obtained gainful employment contributes to poor decision-making. This can lead to violations of the law, ushering them into a system that has been designed to maintain law and order. For certain segments of the population, these circumstances result in their becoming immersed in the penal system. Understanding the circumstances in which many of these fathers are living, we educated them about societal forces that would derail their goals. Fathers residing in impoverished neighborhoods with limited resources often make poor decisions when trying to provide for their families. This is where we go back to the ecosystem, helping them understand the dangers of getting involved in a system that can have an impact on their ability to be a part of their children's lives. Some of this is information they should already know; however, in many instances, what we have found is that they either do not know or do not care. They are attempting to respond to societal influences dictating what they should be doing as fathers.

Incidents of domestic violence: Domestic violence was always one of those situations where we had to help fathers get to the core of the problem. When dealing with infants, toddlers, and preschoolers, when they are engaged in play and issues arise over a toy or access to a slide on the playground, and frustration sets in, we immediately tell the children to use their words.

We also know that when children have difficulty regulating their emotions or challenges with speech, they will lash out, repeating observed behavior, which is to hit. Hitting someone for whatever reason, to control them, to get them to listen to you, or because you feel they, in the moment, deserve to be chastised, is ludicrous. Lashing out is grounded in one's inability to articulate feelings or emotions in a healthy way, helping us understand that hitting is, in fact, a form of communication.

This is where we must help fathers remember that, up to this point in their lives, self-regulation has not been something they have cared to embrace, because, in the communities where they live and work, self-regulation, in some instances, could lead to their demise.

We focused intently on helping them understand the importance of self-regulation and how this was a significant adjustment they needed to make, as it was counterintuitive to the ways in which they had learned to survive in their communities. As one grows older, matures, and begins to understand the difference between acceptable and unacceptable behaviors, they can discern that there are consequences for their behavior, which can remove them from having any influence in their child's life and harm someone they profess to care about.

Getting help is critical if expanded knowledge and understanding of what drives their desire to hit is not manageable. And it was important that they help their children with this issue as well. Another important point we emphasized was that domestic violence was non-negotiable.

I was the benefactor of so many rich conversations and encounters with men who were genuinely interested in and passionate about their role as fathers. When they learned that they could positively influence their children's social, emotional, and cognitive behaviors, they lit up, asked questions, invested in their own learning, studied, and planned thoughtful play interventions with their children.

They would come back and share things they observed and make predictions about their children's future. The individual and group experiences laid the foundation for deeper, more meaningful discussions as we explored the fathering role in greater detail. The success of the Bronx Fatherhood program garnered a great deal of attention throughout the organization, the city, and the lower quadrant of the state. Not only were we running a successful program, but we were also in a unique position to advise our colleagues and other organizations on how to engage men to do similar work.

I was asked to train, both internally and externally, with professionals in various settings who recognized the benefits of increasing their capacity to engage fathers. So, it was not long before we partnered with a sister program within the organization, the Nurse-Family Partnership, which provided similar services to mothers. They requested that I train all their home visitors. They were nurses who conducted weekly home visits with enrolled mothers. They often saw fathers and attempted to engage them; however, they were not meeting with success. So, I was asked to facilitate in-service training for the entire team.

The training went well, and it marked the beginning of integrating our work throughout the agency. I consulted with nurses who reached out for advice on how to build on and use the strategies discussed during the training. In turn, when and if they were successful, they would refer fathers to our program for on-going support and services. It was truly a win-win situation, and it began to make a huge difference in work across both of our programs.

My team and I received an invitation to attend a graduation ceremony at Lincoln Hospital for several moms after they completed the program. We went to show our support for our colleagues and the moms who were graduating. It was a well-organized ceremony, and when it was over, my colleague, Carol Odnoha, the Director of the program, introduced me to a woman from a foundation. She informed me that she had heard a great deal about the work I was doing with the fathers.

Her organization was interested in working with a father's program; however, after visiting several programs in the city, they had not found one that they felt worthy. I extended an invitation, and it was only after that that I learned I was speaking to Kate Fenniman,

Executive Director of the Baby Buggy Foundation. This was Jessica Seinfeld's Family Foundation.

After becoming a mom a few times, Jessica realized how expensive baby clothing and supplies were, and she started this charitable foundation to support parents in need. To be honest, I was not fazed. I met with my team on Monday and informed them of the possibility of the meeting occurring sometime that week. I was packing up, getting ready to leave the office at the end of the day, when I received a call from Kate. She told me Jessica had freed up time on her schedule and asked if it was okay if she came to meet with me and my team before observing the group. I told her I would be delighted to have her join.

Having been in a leadership role for years, I understood the magnitude of the situation, so I called my supervisor to let her know what had transpired and suggested we schedule a call with the development office. Vivian got them on the phone right away, and of course, they wanted to seize the moment, control the narrative, and take this out of my hands. Although this was my first rodeo with a foundation interested in building a relationship with me, I understood, as an experienced leader, not only how to manage the situation but also how to manage up.

I pushed back hard on the agency's proposal. I told them that the foundation was interested in the Bronx Fatherhood Program, not the Visiting Nurse Service of New York, and that the program needed to be our focus at this time. I was fine with them preparing materials about the organization, which I could share if that was their wish. And instead of sending an entire team from the development office, they could send one person to participate in the meeting. They agreed!

Kate and Jessica arrived on time for our scheduled meeting. Jessica was an instant delight. Her mother was a social worker, so she had great insight into the work, the importance of what we were doing, and she was genuinely interested in our formula.

What was our recipe, and why were we meeting with success when the other programs were not able to do the same? I had prepared my team, so they joined us, and one by one, they introduced themselves. They talked about our philosophical approach to the work, how important it was for us to be genuine, the amount of in-service training and professional development we engaged in to keep our skills sharp, and the fact that we utilized social work interns from local colleges and universities to assist with the individual counseling. This was because many of the fathers challenged by their fathers' absence displaced their anger onto their mothers and their romantic partners. Working with female social workers helped them learn to be appropriate in their communication and interaction with women. They were listening intently, and engaged in the conversation, as evidenced by their questions.

The father's group that day was a huge success. We had about fifteen 16 to 24-year-old non-custodial fathers sitting around the table, many of them had their children with them. Not only were they engaged in the group process, but they also appropriately attended to their children and actively participated while taking copious notes. Everyone was on point that night, and it was one of the best groups we had. I had a few minutes to debrief with Jessica and Kate after the meeting. Kate could not contain her joy. Jessica shook my hand, thanked me, and asked me to submit a proposal to her for any immediate need that would help me provide additional services. I assured her that I would.

I worked on the proposal as requested and pushed it up the chain through the appropriate channels within my organization before submitting it to Kate for Jessica's review. My request was modest; I needed additional funding to pay for a Part time - Job Developer and another Project Coordinator. My number came in at around 60K. Leadership within the development office again saw this as an opportunity to request additional funding for the agency at large, modifying my proposal in hopes that the foundation would accommodate. I was not in agreement; however, this was not a battle I could win.

A couple of days after submitting the proposal, Kate scheduled a call so we could discuss it. When I discovered how much the agency requested, I was embarrassed. They changed the proposal to 500k and requested that the additional funding be earmarked for a pediatric palliative care program. When I joined the call, Jessica was on the line as well, and she opened by saying, "David, I've dealt with these situations before; my focus is your program in the Bronx. We can discuss additional support for the program in Queens as well. Send me a proposal with your needs." I thanked her again for her generosity and for understanding.

I called Vivian, informed her of the conversation, and requested her assistance. Within a couple of hours, she told me to submit my original proposal to the foundation. It was not more than a week after I sent the updated proposal that I received a check in the mail that was substantial enough to cover a full-time and a part-time position.

I was delighted, and when I circled back to Kate to thank her and Jessica, I was asked if I would be willing to come to Jessica's for breakfast, where I could meet with a group of women to discuss and share more information about the father's program design and approach to service delivery. I told them I would be delighted, and we coordinated our schedules and set a day to meet.

When I shared this additional request with my supervisor, she was delighted. She had concerns, so she decided to reach out to her supervisor for advice. Once again, there was an internal meeting with leadership staff, including a representative from the CFO's office and the VP of Development. They had ideas about who should accompany me and how the meeting should be structured. I was told that I needed to talk up the entire Children and Family Services Division and seek opportunities for additional funding. I was thinking to myself, they could not be that dense. They decided three staff members from the development office would accompany me. I listened respectfully and then requested permission to speak.

I reminded them that this was in Jessica's home and that there was no way I would attend the meeting with individuals who were not invited. I provided a rational explanation as to why it would be ludicrous for us to attempt to adjust the invitation to satisfy self-serving interests.

I further explained that if we managed this situation responsibly, other opportunities might become available in the future, allowing the foundation to learn more about the organization. I reassured leadership that I would adequately address and respond to their questions. Of course, they had no other alternative than to relent. Losing a battle can feel unsettling, and yet it is so much more rewarding to win the war!

The day came for me to attend the meeting with Jessica and her prestigious group of women. I was in the neighborhood, at a coffee shop around the corner from their Central Park West residence, at least an hour before. There was no way I was going to be late for the meeting.

Perspective is a way of thinking about and understanding, or of formulating, a particular point of view. It is how we see the world, the people around us, and ourselves. With maturity, it changes over time and is something we learn to manage through varied lifetime experiences. If we are smart, we quickly realize that no two perspectives are exactly the same.

This unique viewpoint informs how we live our lives, how we interact with others, and how we move toward our goals. Like many other things in life, we have to contend with, and although it is not right, I am used to being followed around when I enter certain stores, or when I am in a neighborhood where some individuals are inclined to believe I do not belong.

It does not surprise me when and if I encounter an over enthusiastic police officer, who is a doppelganger for Archie Andrews, demonstrating serious concerns not only about my day, but also where I plan on going. The conversation almost always ends with an I.D. check; however when I match these experiences, their aggressive almost excitable energy, with humility, patience, and an intelligent, non-provocative response that equates to the eloquence and sophistication displayed by Dixon, the railroad car porter, I am allowed to continue on my way.

Throughout the week, not unlike the shot heard around the world, several Vice Presidents within the organization reached out to me, offering congratulations and sharing how lucky I was to have the Seinfeld Family Foundation interested in the fathers program. They were celebrating the fact that I was invited into their home. While I recognized and appreciated the significance of it all, I was raised to believe inherently that there is no one on this earth better than me. There are many individuals who are more fortunate, who have been blessed with great fortune, and yet, that is their fortune.

My position on the entire situation was to keep things in perspective, be myself, convey the importance of the work, and leverage any opportunities presented to me to expand the impact we were making. I learned in life through my religious beliefs that it is important to be wary of shadow missions. Biblically speaking, a shadow mission is an authentic mission that has been derailed, often in imperceptible ways. Part of what makes the shadow mission so tempting is that it is usually so closely related to our gifts and passions.

I felt honored and blessed to be able to dialogue with such influential individuals. I recognized and appreciated that they were interested not only in hearing from me but also in learning from me how I was able to be successful doing something they had not been able to witness in other programs in the New York metropolitan area. It is important to recognize that while I was in this position, because of the work that I was doing, it was only by God's grace that I was able to be the one to meet with unprecedented success.

I introduced the conversation about perspective to share a situation that occurred on this day that was unfortunate; however, it turned out to be uneventful, one because of my response, and two because of the compassionate way Jessica handled the situation. She was, and has always been, true to form during my encounters with her, and I will forever be grateful and appreciative of her and her foundation for the genuine interest and support they provided to my program and my dream.

My upbringing and my military experiences ingrained in me that if you are on time, then you are late, so I am rarely, if ever, late. I decided that, on the chance I would be able to meet with Jessica's husband, I would give him a gift, so I took a varsity athletic jacket that the fathers receive upon graduation as a token of appreciation for their generosity. I also stopped by a local floral shop and purchased a dozen long-stemmed yellow roses for Jessica. After all, she had invited me into her home.

It was cold that day, and although I was wearing a suit, I also had on a custom varsity athlete jacket. When I entered the building from the Central Park West entrance, the doorman sent me to the service elevator. I was a male of color, and he assumed that I was a delivery person and not a guest. I could have been angry; however, I was not. He was doing his job to the best of his ability. After all, I am not certain, to be honest, that the Seinfelds had a lot of guests who looked like me.

However, when I arrived at the entrance to the residence, I saw a horrid look on Jessica's face. She welcomed me and immediately showed concern as to why I was on the service elevator. She apologized profusely, then called down to the doorman to share her concern and let him know that other guests would be arriving soon.

I have been in places where breakfast displays covered the spectrum; however, this was something to behold. I already had a cup of coffee and was not much of a breakfast person; however, I filled a small plate with a few items. As I moved over to the couch to sit, Jerry entered, walked over with an outstretched hand, and welcomed me into his home. He was gracious. Jessica shared a little about the work I was doing with him, and he thanked me for coming. We made a bit of small talk, and after a few minutes, he said he had a few things to attend to and was leaving. I gave him the jacket, he thanked me again, and he left the room.

It was surreal. I cannot tell you how many Seinfeld episodes I watched, and there I was, standing in the home of a legend. I would later learn that the fifteen or so women in attendance were among the most powerful in NYC, many of whom were married to several influential men. I must admit, there were so many women there it was hard to remember them all; however, Jessica and Alexandra "Ali" Wentworth stood out.

They were so welcoming and engaging, I felt like we'd known each other for a long time. When the time came, and the room was filled with guests, I shared my story, which took all of 20 minutes, and then it was time for questions and answers. Several women seemed genuinely interested and asked great questions. I responded confidently and reassured them that our goal was to be impactful, helping the fathers make life-sustaining changes. Ali, Jessica, and I talked for quite a while after several women left for other engagements. I sat there listening intently to their conversation, as they discussed plans for what they thought we might be able to do together. They were thinking about having me meet a few other powerful colleagues and possibly appearing on Good Morning America (Ali is married to George Stephanopoulos).

I walked a few city blocks, processing our meeting. Admittedly, I was struggling a bit. This was a great opportunity for the organization and the program; however, it felt as if too much attention was focused on me. It was important that the focus remained on the program, so it was difficult to appreciate the magnitude of what this could potentially mean. I refused to get caught up in a shadow mission. I was immensely grateful; however, the timing was not great because I was going through a very personal trauma at the time that eventually changed the trajectory of my work in New York, which is a story for another time.

Generative Fathering proposes that a vital element in the relationship between fathers and their children, including fathers facilitating attachments or simply connecting with the child in a supportive, lasting relationship. The challenge with this theoretical framework is that it is sometimes misconstrued to proport fathering practices that look a lot like what mothers do with their children. The social construction of gender is the pivotal question that often undermines a father's ability to demonstrate a particular competency with respect to nurturing care in distinct and unique ways that matter to him and the child. Now, because of the work of several dedicated professionals and organizations that support fathers, we are beginning to see a change.

The focus shifted to the unique roles and behaviors of fathers and what men bring to the table. Practitioners must see themselves as advocates for fathers in the same way they see themselves as advocates for mothers. They are both parents, so why do we view them any differently? Whether it's a one-on-one conversation, a webinar, or an in-person professional development event, I say to practitioners, if you find yourself having difficulty communicating with and engaging a father; the next time you have an opportunity to do so, imagine for a moment how comfortable and intentionally different you would be if it were a mom standing in front of you demonstrating an inability to connect. Are we certain it is not our own assumptions and biases preventing our success?

Another indication that I was navigating a unique path was when I was asked to return to the Clinical Institute at the Jewish Board of Children and Family Services as an adjunct. A couple of times each year, I would facilitate a fatherhood training to either the incoming or outgoing class. It was an honor to be able to speak with colleagues who were not only at the height of their careers but also in unique positions to structure programming that was inclusive of fathers. On the heels of one of these presentations, another mentor and respected colleague, Rebecca Shamoon-Shanok, asked if I could meet with her briefly afterwards. We took the elevator to her office after my training session, and she offered me the opportunity to train with her as part of a course she was developing for use in several states. Normally, I take time to evaluate the merits of offers such as this; however, my respect for her and her body of work led me to accept the offer before I thoroughly evaluated what it would entail.

Within a few weeks, we were in Palm Beach County, FL, at a Parent Child Center for a full day of staff development. Attendees were teachers and practitioners who wanted to better understand the work and process of facilitating fathers' groups, as well as the nuances of dyadic work with fathers and their children. It was to this day one of the highlights of my career as an educator and an advocate for father engagement.

Our objectives for the full-day training experience focused on ensuring that the participants would:

o Self-assess their attitudes towards fathers

o Gain the ability to establish essential connections with fathers

o Gain the capacity to erase subconscious barriers to engagement

o Become more comfortable including fathers in their thinking and their work,

o Utilize more process-oriented interventions

o Work from a position of optimism vs cynicism

o Become familiar with reasons that fathers may be evasive

o Become able to think of ways to address "evasiveness"

o Become inspired to include fathers (as we do mothers) in ways that work for them and their children's growth

o Become more knowledgeable about ways to help fathers feel comfortable and competent with their child, their child's mom, educators, and other staff working in the childcare programs their child attends

o Become familiar with criteria to include or exclude fathers in family or dyadic work

This opportunity illustrated how the tentacles of the work were beginning to spread into areas where impactful changes were needed, and I was partially responsible. One other point that I think is worth mentioning. Because of the diverse approaches organizations were using to reach and support families, I was also scaffolding my knowledge on how to provide support to fathers through the home-based option respectfully. This was an essential component of the early childhood education services programs provided. I was instrumental in helping staff support fathers and families. My experience yet again placed me in a position where I was asked to present at a Home Visiting Conference.

By now, I was a sought-after presenter, becoming increasingly comfortable speaking in front of large groups. The attendance at this conference was outstanding. Coordinators, Home Visitors, and early literacy professionals, traveled from Massachusetts, Illinois, California, Washington State, and as far away as Dublin, Ireland, to participate in the Conference. The workshops had participants learning about everything from understanding autism to serving homeless families to ensuring staff followed appropriate safety protocols during home visits. One of the workshops, of note, titled "Involving Fathers/Men: Creating a Culture of Inclusion."

According to one participant, "The workshop helped us appreciate getting fathers involved and appreciate the role they play. Society overlooks fathers and that is not a luxury educators have. The presenter (David Jones) was amazing," said Lydia Lester from the Horry County South Carolina site.

These conversations and this enhanced thinking led to another pivotal shift in our approach to supporting fathers. What will it take for us to forget our usual way of doing something so that we can learn a new and sometimes better approach?

And, what has our discipline taught us? How does this enable or prevent us from being successful in our engagement efforts?

• Our discipline has taught us to assess, evaluate, and support fathers/families based upon our training. Inexperienced clinicians and practitioners cling to theoretical frameworks that shape how we use the skills we learned in pursuit of our degrees. The more experienced clinician or practitioner takes time to evaluate and assess the client's particular situation, their history, how they have navigated past relationships, and the relationship they are attempting to build together.

Every successful intervention is fluid, time-sensitive, and based on how the relationship is evolving. Yes, there will be competency considerations, as well as limitations when considering the client/father's ability or inability to follow through and complete tasks. However, if and when the relationship is genuine, and the practitioner follows the father's lead or, at a minimum, paces their intervention, they will be more aligned with the father's capacity to respond appropriately. If such is not the case, and the relationship has evolved to the place where it needs to be, the client will not have any problems discussing where they are having difficulty meeting the goals.

• As practitioners, the question is, what do we need to abandon or unlearn? I recommend sitting with discomfort, staying in the moment longer than our training suggests, and allowing derailments of the structured process to lead to purposeful pivots and shifts. As we so often do with infants and toddlers, look to the father to assess whether what you are doing is working. If it is not working, it will reveal itself, whether it is your discovery or the father telling you.

• Working with fathers begins with the belief that engagement is possible. Just as we believe in our experience and training, degree in hand, we rely on experience with fathers to guide our approach to the work. We must also believe in the fathers we are hoping to engage. We must believe that not only is engagement possible, but we must also believe that fathers have the capacity to partner with us to define and outline how to better support them. This becomes the foundation of all our efforts, and once fathers are clear that we are investing in them in support of their role, they tend to get on board.

The question is, how do we view fathers?

- Fathers are Individuals, which is defined as a single human being distinct from a group, class, or family. What does this mean for them, and more importantly, what does it mean for us? Is this even something that we consider during our encounters with them? Because our services and support are tied to a particular objective, to get them to do something, or to engage differently, we are looking at them contextually with respect to their role in the family system and not necessarily who they are as individuals. And yet, they are individuals with their own historical past and unique experiences that either create opportunities to rise to the level of our expectations or present challenges. Unless we have a conversation with them, we will never know.

- As parents, they have their own lived experiences, beginning with how they were parented within their family of origin. Whether those experiences were positive or not, they bring these experiences to the table with them and unless we engage them in meaningful dialogue about the beliefs and practices, we will be applying a Eurocentric approach to our efforts to get them to behave in ways that may or may not be aligned with who they are or with what they want for their child/family. And in cases where their involvement is mandated, and they have no choice, know there will be greater reticence. It is important to remember that, regardless of their initial status, in some instances, failure to comply can permanently alter their lives.

- As 'co-parents,' they are locked in the best-case scenario in a symbiotic relationship with their child's mother, and they are navigating and negotiating an approach to parenting that must be aligned. Communication and compromise are essential, as they must make daily decisions about their children's educational, religious, health, and nutrition experiences, which may require collaboration. Depending on their beliefs and practices, this can be easy if the parents are able to agree. What we do know is that, in most instances when we meet these families, that is not necessarily the case. Our charge then is to help empower and sometimes disempower parents to reach a place where they can appreciate the other parent's perspective, do what is in the child's best interest, and align their parenting goals, expectations, and practices.

- As contributing members of society, there is an expectation that fathers have learned the rules governing how one should behave. Abiding by the laws, working, taking care of one's responsibilities, paying taxes, and giving back to the community in some shape, form, or fashion is the expectation. What happens when one lacks a basic understanding of an ecosystem and their place within it? What happens when someone has had a compromised past when they were a child? They are enveloped in unresolved traumatic experiences, preventing them from skillfully and successfully navigating society. Are they easily forgiven? I would think not, especially if we had not taken the time to learn about their past.

- How about their level of comfort navigating institutions? We are or should be aware of the pitfalls and traps that are there, i.e., the pipeline to prison, systems that seek to incarcerate as opposed to helping young men make good decisions in life. Fathers must navigate institutions such as education, health, criminal justice, and social service programs to gain access to their child or children.

- They have never been comfortable within these systems, and in many instances, they have not had good outcomes. It is our responsibility to recognize these past experiences and help fathers understand why they must move differently within these systems.

- What needs to be changed, modified, or enhanced about the way we communicate with fathers? I pose this to practitioners because this is a question that should be at the forefront of our minds anytime we engage a father. I constantly return to the example, if this were a mother who came in for services, seeking assistance, how would you engage her? What questions would you ask? What would be important for you to know to accurately assess her level of need and provide services and support that would address those specific needs? To summarize, fathers are individuals, they are parents, they are co-parents, and they will at some point become contributing members of society. We engage them based on their cognitive capacity, emotional state, and willingness to comply with our request to initially provide information demonstrating that they qualify for services and then meet specific program expectations. This requires a level of competency that satisfies our expectations, which will then allow them access to their child or children again.

Defining Families Today

"Whoever walks in integrity walks securely, but he who makes his ways crooked will be found out."

Proverbs 10:9

What about the ever-changing definition of family? While this list is not all-encompassing, what we are attempting to illustrate is that how people define themselves and their respective families continues to evolve. It is essential that families, whatever the configuration, provide consistency, stability, and support for their children. Our focus should be on contributing to and supporting the best environment for the child. Whether it's both parents or one parent, the goal is to have individuals who are mature and able to make decisions that support the child's social, emotional, and cognitive development.

- We have single-parent families. A single parent is unmarried, widowed, legally separated, or divorced and not remarried.

The single-parent household can be headed by a mother, a father, a grandparent, an uncle, or an aunt. According to the Pew Research Center, between 25 to 30 percent of children under the age of eighteen in the U.S. live in a single-parent household.

- Two-parent heterosexual families. Nuclear families, also known as elementary or traditional families, consist of two parents, usually married or common law, and their children.

- LGBTQ+ same sex parenting families. Same sex parenting is the parenting of children by same sex couples consisting of gays or lesbians who are often in civil partnerships, domestic partnerships, civil unions, or same sex marriages.

- Blended families. A blended family, also known as a stepfamily, is a family formed when two people come together and bring a child or children from previous relationships.

- Multi-generational families are families that are comprised of several generations of family members that could include grandparents, parents, children, and grandchildren.

Fathers, who are they really? If we are serious about our efforts to engage fathers in meaningful ways, we must collect data on them in the same manner that we collect data on mothers. We are skilled at digging deep when it comes to exploring a mother's past in an effort to best understand how we can provide support. We are attempting to determine whether there are limitations that could adversely affect their ability to contribute to the process, while at the same time leveraging any potential strengths they may possess. An important question we can ask ourselves is, what do we know about a father's history that we have not learned from others?

- Fathers are individuals with their own unique backgrounds and experiences. There is a lot of pressure on them to successfully navigate that fact alone, not to mention the task of understanding and evolving in their role as men.

- Fathers are parents, and their capacity to evolve into this aspect of the role is contingent upon several factors and grounded in their own experience being parented. Factors like educational and employment history, their relationship with the other parent, and whether they have access to their children.

- If a father has negated or neglected his role as an engaged father, is not gainfully employed, and is still attempting to find his way, do we view him as a contributing member of society? What are our normal programmatic expectations? Regardless of where he is and what his experience with institutions has been, we expect conformity. In many instances, for these men, conformity, something most programs expect, can be an initial deterrent until a relationship and trust have been established.

When fathers are supported in their capacity to grow in the areas mentioned above, they can achieve desirable outcomes. This is where practitioners need to revisit the self-assessment process, honestly confronting their own strengths and limitations as it relates to engaging men. It requires practitioners to take a hard look at their capacity and motivations for doing this work, as well as revisit past experiences with men in their own lives, which can contribute to or preclude their success.

- Although moms can provide a wealth of information and, in most instances, are the conduit to obtaining information about the fathers, they can also impede access as gatekeepers, preventing informed engagement, which can be problematic.

- It is important to professionally align with fathers. We have an obligation to meet them where they are and work with them based on their capacity to get to a different place.

- It is important to remember that if practitioners are working in an early childhood program or some other early childhood setting, 49-50% of the children will potentially be male. This is important because if staff have unresolved issues with adult males, there is a chance that this can influence their interactions with male children.

- Practitioners must be willing to continuously self-assess because, at various intervals, things will surface that will challenge our capacity to comfortably engage fathers. What happens when the relationship you so desire with a father reaches that point, and now there is an unhealthy attraction to the father? How does one manage this, or what do they do with these feelings? What happens if a father exceeds appropriate boundaries and crosses a line?

Couple the content referenced above with Program Engagement mandates. What do we expect, and are we creating a welcoming environment?

- What expectations do we hold for fathers' participation?

- What is our position on conformity vs. flexibility when fathers walk through our doors?

- How skilled are we at relating to these men, given their unique culture, and how does that contribute to authentic engagement?

- What have we done to ensure our physical environment is welcoming for fathers?

- What have we done to ensure all staff who might encounter fathers have been adequately trained?

MAN CHILD

"I'm six feet tall
stand down
or so you will lay,
is usually all I have to say.
I'm the only "Mother"
you see standing on stage
yet you know little of the man
that I am,
locked in a cage.
that's who I become,
when I'm filled with rage.

Without any regard
I'm out of control
ushering someone closer
to a meeting with their soul.

Once out of the box
I'm helpless can't you see
he's dictating my life
with audacity,

Speaking for me
Walking for me
Talking for me

skillfully fighting,
like the martial artist I've become
changing all that is the essence of me
or the essence of the man, I wanted to be

I recall…….
Mamma telling me,
"Get that girl out of here, Trina's on her way
Tell her to shut up and listen to what you say!
You're the boss don't take that; boy be a man!"

So here I am
with time on my hands
to think and reflect, to understand
I never knew my father
what did you expect

that my life would be different,
that somehow it would change,
how is that possible
when you taught me the game?
It was you who refused
to give me his name.
This was strategic,
this was your stand,
you didn't give me a change
to come up with a plan.
And when I asked
you of his memory
you shrugged your shoulders
said, "Son let me be."
Mamma, look at me now,
I'm in a cold dark cell
my soul is messed up
my body just a shell
the thing I discovered
it's not a surprise
I was just like him
in stature and size
all those years
you couldn't see me
you saw my father
and the man he couldn't be
all attributes you instilled in me
I'm nothing like
I aspired to be

I know you did your best
Giving all that you could
And for that I am grateful
Yeah, it's all good
The things that you taught me
I now understand
I'm lost and I'm lonely
A broken man."

Revisiting Engagement
Barriers/Obstacles

I want to take a moment to place additional emphasis on some of the barriers and obstacles that can adversely impact engagement.

- It is important to remember that many of the men you will encounter have not had adequate road maps. What I am referring to are individuals who have modeled successful behavior patterns when executing fathering practices to fulfil their responsibilities.

- Given the lack of role models, it makes sense that many will lose their way due to a lack of preparation. It is a known fact that a significant percentage of what we learn in early life is a direct result of what is modeled for us. It is hard to be what they cannot see.

- Many men will require attitude and behavioral adjustments. The only way to successfully assist them with this is by first observing the behavior over time and then leaning on trusting relationships, which take time to develop.

- It took a while before I could fully appreciate and understand the power of the maternal relationship and what that can do for young men. It can be a contributing factor related to their success and/or failure when it comes to embracing the role. Given the data on father absence, in many instances, it is mothers who end up rearing the children fathers leave behind. When mothers can get past the broken promise, prioritize, and accomplish their own unmet goals, they are in a much better position to guide and provide for their children. When this does not happen, and they are unable to get past the broken relationship, they often struggle to accomplish their own goals. As a result, their capacity to provide support and guidance for their children suffers. What is even worse is that if their own physical and mental health is compromised, they can negatively influence their children, poisoning them against the other parent, and in some cases, damage them further.

- We have historically focused on the implications of paternal absence, and data have helped us better understand how important positive paternal presence can be. A father's absence remains a barometer for future success and is something that must be understood. Fathers who have successfully dealt with or come to terms with their paternal history fare much better in the fathering role when it is their turn. However, initially, without the requisite support, they either embrace the role vociferously or they run because they believe they are not equipped to fulfill the responsibility.

- Many of these men will be impatient and will want you to alter the course of their life right away, even though they might not be prepared. This requires a juggling act, where you provide appropriate supports and, at the same time, help fathers understand the important skill of patience and the need to establish goals they can accomplish before significant, life-sustaining changes can be made.

- A key strategy, and one I might add, that becomes an on-ramp to developing trusting relationships is the program's ability to address a concrete need.

How men with a compromised past sometimes present themselves when they walk through your doors.

- Angry

- Avoidant

- Depressed

- Lack Confidence

- Prone to Violence

- Risk Takers

Revisiting the rationale for engaging in this work, looking at current data. Single-parent households have more than tripled since 1960.

- 18.3 million children live without a father in the home (1 in 4)

- As of 2019, a staggering 23% of children lived with one parent and no other adults, which was over three times the global average of 7%, according to Pew Research.

- The statistics are even more staggering for Black children, with 50% living with a single mother (Livingston, 2018).

- Single mothers (U.S. Census Bureau, 2022) lead eighty percent of single-parent homes

- Sadly, fatherless families are four times more likely to raise children in poverty (U.S. Census, 2020)

- Children from single-parent families are twice as likely to suffer from mental health and behavioral problems as those living with married parents

- Seventy percent of youth in state-operated facilities were from single-parent homes

- Children with an actively engaged father perform much better in school; some data shows that they are 33% less likely to repeat a class and 43% more likely to get 'As' in school.

- In a study of fifty-six school shootings, only 10 of the shooters (18%) were raised in a stable home with both biological parents. Eighty-two percent grew up in either an unstable family environment or grew up without both biological parents together.

- 63% of youth suicides

- 71% of high school dropouts

- 66% of juvenile incarcerations

- 72% of adolescent murderers and 70% of long-term prison inmates come from fatherless homes

- 90% of homeless and runaway youth

New Era Fathers

Fathers who can adequately position themselves to engage, early, often, and maintain a level of consistency is a good definition of a New Era father. How are we operationalizing New Era fathers? What does that look like today?

They are not overly concerned with archaic gender prescribed roles, and they are responsive and knowledgeable about child development, developmentally appropriate interactions and care, and they are focused on increasing their capacity to respond to all their child's caregiving needs.

When I refer to New Era fathers, I mean fathers making pivotal shifts to be not only fully engaged but also fully present. They, in most instances, refuse to adhere to gender prescribed roles, engaging in practices geared towards their children's holistic well-being. They are consistently finding ways to increase their competence, resulting in more thoughtful and intentional parent-child interactions and practices.

- They have no fear of the mirror

- They are open to learning

- They confront and embrace challenges

- They acknowledge their fears

- They are not afraid to ask for help

- They admit mistakes

- They demonstrate (show) affection

- They communicate (talk to their child)

- They are curious about their child's development

- They are willing to make sacrifices for their children

- They love their children openly and freely

- They model respectable behavior

With respect to fathering tasks:

- They take their child to well-baby appointments,

- They care for their child while the child's mother is at work overnight/weekends

- They keep copies of important documents, i.e., birth certificate, health records, allergy information

- They keep important telephone numbers handy

- They meet with their child's teacher,

- They take responsibility and are invested in the child's education/learning,

- They prioritize their child/children

- They willingly contribute to their children's financial well-being

- They learn to understand, embrace, and appreciate their role as fathers They share common experiences with their child

- They teach children about history, family, and the world They maintain a safe, secure, and stable home environment They are willing to expand their parenting knowledge

- They plan child-focused activities

- They model appropriate behavior

- They understand their role as a teacher

- They are concerned about attachment and bonding

Recognizing Strengths in Differently Abled Children

Irving Harris said, "The first few months of life are not a rehearsal. It's the real show." Zero to Three Apr/May 1998 Vol. 18 no. 5, Pushing Kids into the River. The work we do daily, observing, assessing, and interacting with children, should put us in a constant state of wonder. It's easy to imagine all the wonderful possibilities that exist just after a child is born. Then imagine a parent's worst nightmare! When children are born with some sort of significant developmental delay, there is a psychological shift that many parents undergo, which makes it challenging for them to accept and even more challenging for them to functionally respond to the needs of the child.

Without the support and services to help them deal with the initial shock and grief associated with the real versus the ideal child, it is sometimes difficult for parents to move forward. Many resort to living in a state of constant denial. Gaither conducted some research in 1997 with neonates, which looked at fathers' ability to interact with their children who were in the neonatal intensive care unit.

When children are born with developmental challenges, in many instances, mothers internalize the experience differently, frequently grappling with feelings of blame and shame. Fathers, when available and supported, can respond to their children's needs much more rapidly than mothers. Mothers of pre-term babies and children born with developmental challenges may themselves be ill after giving birth; consequently, fathers of pre-term infants are compelled to pick up even more slack in early caretaking responsibilities. Men, in some ways, don't initially internalize the challenges babies face as something they are responsible for; they see them as obstacles they have to respond to.

I do not believe they are suffering less than mothers; however, they often are able to functionally engage as medical providers call upon them to do so. Many fathers have shared that medical professionals have told them it is good for the child when they are physically present, touching, and learning to care for them, so they step up and accept that their partners are not able to do so at the time. It is important that practitioners recognize the psychic reorganization that occurs when a family has, for nine months, imagined they would have a particular child, and when the child turns out to be other than what they imagined, there is a deep sense of loss.

It is oxymoronic in that there is the death of the idealized child and the birth of the real child, which compromises the process of acceptance vs. denial, requiring support and clinical intervention. This creates an opportunity to help parents accept and be open to learn how they can positively impact and support their child's developmental needs. Children will be able to optimize their development through loving and supportive relationships with caregivers and a sensitive, responsible therapist, despite the limitations they will face.

The end goal here is to help them on their acceptance journey, walking alongside parents as they move from disbelief and denial to acceptance, understanding, and advocacy, maximizing their child's potential.

"If anyone had told me when you were born that you would never read, never write, or never carry on a normal conversation, I wouldn't have been able to handle it."

"Truthfully, I was crushed for a long, long time when I found out that you had autism." - Robert A. Naseef, Ph.D.

Focusing on Strategies

Responsive strategies begin with staff revisiting a father's history. It is important to remember that fathering practices are influenced by the journey beginning with one's family of origin. How fathers were raised informs their initial understanding of the role. If they had positive experiences of good parenting, they might have something they can use as a foundation for their approach to the parenting role. Otherwise, they are often starting from nothing. A few important questions for consideration:

- What was the impact of their experiences with their fathers, brothers, or other men in their lives?

- What role did their mother and or maternal figures play in responding to questions about their father if he was not present?

- Have they adequately dealt with the challenges surrounding their relationship with their father or the lack thereof?

- It is often necessary for practitioners to help fathers remove the blinders from their eyes. A cautionary tale, something most clinicians understand, it is important to take great care in how we illuminate and help fathers remove their blinders. The blinders they rely on help them cling to defense mechanisms, preventing them from coming into close kinship with painful experiences. We also must be sure we are prepared to help fathers find other coping strategies. As practitioners, it is important for us to rethink our expectations to ensure they are not unrealistic, unfair, or benefiting us more than the father.

Partnering with Fathers

Another essential strategy is our capacity to view families as partners. We would be nothing without the families, and in many instances, they would not be able to actualize their goals without our assistance. If we truly value fathers as partners along the way, we will ensure that fathers are aware that we are following their lead. Sometimes we must be strategic in how we guide them along the way. We can do this by:

- Investing a little more time in the beginning, which will most often save time overall.

- Acknowledging and remaining aware that, although extremely powerful, we are a temporary influence in a child's/father's life. How significant would it be if we were to leave most of that influence with them in some capacity?

- Knowing that it is not until we can challenge our preexisting beliefs about men that we will be effective at including them in aspects of service provision as it relates to their children.

- Staff should not assume they do not want to be involved.

- When evaluating how to best include fathers, believe they are or have the capacity to become experts when it comes to their children.

- Recognizing that involvement can look quite different than what we expect or can see.

- Sharing in the small success of their involvement, as it is not unlike all other developmental trajectories, good fathering evolves over time.

- Practitioners draw upon multiple disciplines that shape our approach to the work.

- Recognize that our journey towards our discipline is imprinted upon our memory.

- Keep in mind that "We are, of course, professionals, aren't we?" We are not perfect; we, too, are fallible and capable of making mistakes. Practitioners encompass multiple disciplines that shape our approach to the work.

The Road of Life is Paved with Good Intentions

What professionals have good intentions when they make the decision to engage clients. Different circumstances dictate what must get done. Initial intake meetings with clients can color the complexion of future encounters. We understand some behaviors are allowed, and others are frowned upon. It is our charge to be patient, observant, and respectful with fathers. This does not always happen; however, when I first meet with a client, I try to imagine what would make this situation work for me if I were sitting on the other side of the room. So, a few helpful strategies:

- During initial contact, be sensitive to the fact that in most cases, fathers are extremely nervous.

- Be compassionate and consider what shapes the lens through which we view fathers.

- Remain vigilant, paying attention to the things we have not considered, like our own biases, blind spots, and micro-aggressions.

It is also important to take stock and consider a few words about privilege:

- How does privilege show up in our work?

- Fathers are more than what is written about them in their case records.

- It is important to remember that fathers wear several hats as individuals, parents, co-parents, and members of society.

- Take the time to really see the whole person standing in front of you.

- Walk a "minute" in their shoes.

- Commit to creating that Culture of Inclusion.

- Unlearn some of what our discipline has taught us.

- Believe in the capacity of fathers.

- Collect information about fathers.

- Address concrete needs en route to building a trusting relationship

- Expect their involvement and then just watch what happens.

- Recognize the learning curve, i.e., they are willing to learn, grow, and partner with you.

- Survive the test because it is sure to come.

Here, it's important to expand upon the final bullet, explaining what I mean by "the test." When clients are in the early stages of working with helping professionals, they are reluctant to fully engage. It can seem as if they are intentionally attempting to sabotage their own success. However, client "testing" the commitment of a helping professional, while not a formal process, is a client's evaluation of the professional's dedication and engagement in the helping relationship. This can involve observing the professional's actions, interactions, and adherence to professional ethics, and it is crucial for the client to feel respected and supported. Things like their:

- Ability to listen empathetically,

- Willingness to provide guidance and support,

- Ability to establish a positive, collaborative, trusting relationship,

- Ensuring interventions are thoughtful, intentional, and aligned with established goals.

A client's perception of a professional's commitment is a multifaceted assessment. The test considers the professionals' ethical conduct, active engagement, relationship-building skills, and the effectiveness of their interventions in supporting the clients' goals.

Bringing it All Together

In my father's house are many rooms. If it were not so, would I
have told you that I go to prepare a place for you?"
John 14:2 "

The reason so many fathers are navigating this journey is due to a lack of role models, which I sometimes refer to as road maps. Fathers standing up and learning to take responsibility for their children and families, thinking of themselves as fathers first, informs every decision they make. The concept of roadmaps is personally motivating for me, having grown up without my father. In some respects, it was about me and my struggle for personal identification, fulfilment, social and emotional healing, a deeper understanding of who I was, and cognitive growth. It is about navigating the unknown, embracing complexity, and appreciating that the things I thought were preventing my success were not really obstacles at all.

I had to change my perspective on life to come to grips with who I was in the world while discovering my purpose. Once I was able to embrace this self-discovery process and form a comfort level with the complexity, I began to grow. My mind, now spongelike, expanded, opening the door to possibility. It was only then that I realized that I was ready for the task at hand, resulting in my accepting that this journey was chosen for me. My lack of preparation prepared me for the task! I just had to be obedient.

From a historical perspective we are often led to believe that the three "Ps" define a male's position in the family. Which is his ability to procreate, provide for and protect his family. If he was successful in these areas, then his role was complete. Years ago, there was nothing that required or asked that fathers participate in childrearing or responded to the emotional needs of his offspring. Ergo, any request or demand for him to do so would have been a shift in the natural order. There are some aspects of this which still holds true today. I am not a historian yet; I am always open for a good lesson.

However, one thing that I have learned is "His-story," is often presented with a twist of lemon. If one were to research the evolution of man's role in the family with respect to childrearing practices across ethnicities and various cultures throughout the world, one would see that men have played a far more important and versatile role than what is traditionally believed here in America.

In Africa, within traditional Corral systems, according to Madhubuti (1990) "The African father was intimately involved in raising his children, especially the male children. Fathers passed on skills such as food gathering, hunting, knowledge of medicine, building houses, public dwellings, and military science to their sons." In the end our goal is a respectful alliance/partnership with fathers/families that allow us the unique experience of joining them along their journey.

Once we establish trusting relationships with fathers, we can have real conversations. They will allow us to show them how to do things, they will show us things they can do, and they will appreciate it when we share with them that we are human, that we face similar challenges and struggles. It is also important for us to be open to possibilities resulting in meaningful outcomes.

In doing so we create pathways and spaces for the magic to happen. The magic that I am referring to is watching fathers transition from self-explicatory ineptitude to increased competency in their attitudes, behavior, knowledge, and capacity to interact and engage with their children in developmentally appropriate ways.

It is important that we try to communicate with individuals efficiently and effectively in ways that consistently demonstrate that their child is the priority. And finally, they are able to weather the storm, navigate adversarial systems, and difficult co-parenting relationships for the sake of their child/children. When we have done our due diligence, creating that culture of inclusion, we can pull into the driveway, park and say at least for today we have completed our journey.

Earlier I described the structure for father's support groups, and some of the things I believe contributes to successful facilitation. I neglected to discuss in detail an important aspect of this work that will help you fully appreciate this next story. It is about how to skillfully navigate conformity, expectations, and patience with the process. It is important to reiterate that both father's programs were voluntary, however we did on occasion receive a few mandated referrals through our collaboration with family court.

Leon came to the program voluntarily. And although he was only 19 years of age at the time, he had a high school diploma, and he was working preparing for the birth of his daughter. After enrolling in the Bronx Fatherhood Program, he came willingly. Our groups started promptly at 6:00pm on Tuesday's and Thursdays. Most of the attendees were in the meeting room no later than 5:45pm. Leon would arrive at 6:15pm, his MP-3 playing his music loud, and it would take him a good ten to fifteen minutes to settle into the group. It was distracting; however, we carried on.

What is most important about this is while the goal was to have him arrive on time and participate in a similar fashion as the other fathers, allowing him the flexibility to settle in, grab his food, pull out his notetaking materials and join the group when he was ready was key. Our goal was to ensure he benefitted from the knowledge we shared and that he felt welcome. What I did not want to do was apply pressure on him to get to the group before 6:00pm if that was not feasible. I did not want him to feel as if we were policing his time.

The interesting thing is when we began talking about caring for a newborn, a father's role as a teacher and mentor for their child or children, and the fact that this program was dedicated to building the knowledge base of young fathers, he perked up. He tuned in, started asking really great questions. And in asking these questions, you started to see things being revealed to him as he was making comparisons between his own upbringing and what we were talking about in the groups.

His attitude changed and he rearranged his work schedule so he could make it to the group on time. I did not have to say anything to him about his time. It was our flexibility with conformity, and our patience with the process that said welcome in a language he understood!

This is how he described the Bronx Fatherhood Program: *"You are going to go in there; you are going to hold hands. We guys, we are going to sit together, we are going to sing camp songs and have corny laughter. For me, it was when David began describing the program, talking about how it was based on helping young fathers it appealed to me. It immediately drew my attention because I was a young father."* L. Britton

To this day, I am still amazed at what transpired, how he managed the situation, and how he reached out to and consulted with his resources (his caseworker), to focus, to self-regulate, and to be intentionally different when it counted most. Here is Leon's story.

Leon's Story

Me and Rosa had been going through a couple of problems. It was just a big battle; you know, so I was like, respectfully, "I need a break, can I have my space?" At the time, she was pregnant, and we just were not getting along. She responded, "Sure," with an attitude. At that time, my best friend, my right-hand man, was this guy named Mark. I got a text message on my phone from Mark saying, "Yo Leon, I've got to talk to you." And he said, "No disrespect, Lee, but I have feelings for Rosa. I just thought that you should know." My mind just went blank. Like, what!? So, I said, "Are you out of your mind, bro? Do you want me to kill you? Are you serious? Matter of fact, do you know what? I am just going to come to your job. I will holler at you in a few." Click, I hung up the phone and got the knife out of the kitchen.

Before I went back to the break room, we had just gone over the unit of anger management, just gotten over it. Just gotten over the triggers, the things that can trigger you. Just gone over the meaning of anger, and the anger response, which is an instinctive response to a threat of external stimuli. So, I really gave it some thought. You know? I think about it; I think about it. So, I went to his job, and I said, "You know what? You are in front of me now. What is the deal, bro? Speak your piece." He said, "Yo, Lee, yo,

I (stuttering) You know, me and Rachel we broke up, you know. And I see how you are with Rosa.

You guys are always good together. You guys are always happy. I want that." I laughed. I was like, "That is it? That's, you just want somebody to take care of you, bro?" So, I looked at him, straight in the eye, and I said, "You know what, bro? I forgive you." In that moment, I had to show him how much of a man I was and how much of a man he was not.

When his outreach worker came to me and shared this story, I was numb. Leon was inches away from completely derailing his life, and he was able to slow down, reflect, and make a decision that men in their 30s and 40s seem incapable of making. He was able to draw upon some of the timely and relevant information covered in the group, enabling him to be intentionally different. Thinking back on some of my individual conversations with Leon, it was clear to me that he was special. He has taken his own experience growing up with his father as a barometer. And I think if you ask him, he had a good relationship with his father until he hit his adolescent years, and that's when things became a little bit tumultuous.

One afternoon, he shared, "My relationship with my real dad has been spotty. And I will never forget this, he said, "If something was to ever go wrong with you, you just messed up completely, I'll make another one of you." You know, he has five kids."

Leon wants to position himself so he does not have a bad experience. He loves his daughter; he is a great father. He was preparing for her and providing for her in ways that men much older still cannot for their children. He had so much that was inherently good about him when he walked in the door that this was a great situation for him to come into, because the educational piece was what he did not have.

I grew up in a family that was extremely competitive. We participated in sports year-round. Our love language was expressed through sports activities. With that in mind, I would like to share a few things using the analogy of sports, or a reference to the Olympic Games. People participate in sports for competition, physical exertion, and the love of a particular activity. When observing them, one could see the physical exertion, the look on their faces, the grunts, or the tension in their foreheads, and wonder why anyone would engage in such a grueling activity. Yet, if you talk with any athlete, they will tell you, "Game time" is the only opportunity they have to demonstrate just how hard they worked.

It is a test of their own will against other competitors to explore whether or not their hard work has paid off. In our work with fathers/families, we let the games begin when we are able to establish trust and trust ourselves, when we are able to let go against our better judgment and take risks, keeping our composure even when we are unsure. It is in those moments of uncertainty that we often bump up against perfection. Perfection in our work is our ability to dance that delicate dance, providing the requisite guidance and support. It is a father's responsibility to see and to follow our lead when only moments before they were blind. It is incumbent upon them to listen when all they want to do is talk, and to be able to ask for additional support when they are unsure.

These are the signs that the proverbial torch has been lit and that the games have truly begun. This work is grueling. And, similar to the athletes referenced above, we will grunt, get physically exerted, sometimes fight through injuries, and, in some instances, we might want to give up.

This is where we draw upon our training, course correct as appropriate, tap into our resilience, and press on. If we are able to do so, we will walk away with a sense of gratification and personal satisfaction because we were able to finish.

Similarly, as it relates to this work, this is something that only a mature practitioner is able to experience. There is a sense of accomplishment where everyone involved, fathers and their children, can believe that things are going to be okay.

As I bring this story to a close, I feel compelled to say a few things about the work we did, what we were able to accomplish, and ways in which the work can be improved. This evidence-based model can be enhanced in a few areas. I think reworking paternal images and helping fathers heal the wounded father within are essential elements that deserve further attention. It resonates throughout the conceptual model; however, it needs to be expanded upon. This approach takes time and a significant amount of emotional investment, which may be challenging for some practitioners.

At a time when much of the work lends itself to boundaries and optimal distance, it takes skills to negotiate relationships of this magnitude. This comes with experience, commitment, intense supervision, and professional development. There are broad implications for doing this work in the manner suggested, which contributes to improved outcomes for children, families, and society at large.

An important lesson I learned during this process is that the relationships fathers have with their mothers are an intense area of concern that needs additional focus, as many of the fathers I have worked with have more maternal than paternal instincts and baggage.

Often, they conflict with their mothers, which can inform and influence their sense of masculinity, ego functioning, and may impair their perception of and relationships with women. If you made it this far, then it is my belief that the reward is yours, because you have successfully, vicariously, navigated years of hands-on experience of what it is like and of the important considerations when choosing to engage and work with fathers. In many respects, it can and will feel like a mission impossible; however, should you choose to accept it, the reward at the end of the journey will be yours.

I SPEAK FOR THE BOYS

I speak for the boys
African American
An Oxymoron true
I speak for the boys
How about you
I speak for the boys
Tired and alone
I speak for the boys
When no one is at home
I speak for the boys
Craving attachment
Seeking quality care

I speak for the boys
Asking why nobody's there
to answer their questions
Listen to their eyes
When they speak of honest dreams
Not focused on promised skies
To guide and support
Show them you care
Saying even when I'm not present

I'll always be there
To educate them of the pitfalls
Disappointments and traps
the gift of resilience
Their ancestors' maps
the audacity of hope
the ability to care
To think about others
Learning to share
I speak for the boys Long since
forgotten about
I speak for the boys
Who will one day get out

I speak for the boys
Lost inside grown men
Now that I think about it
I speak for them again
I speak for the boys
Who have done their part to
abolish these statistics
Thank you from the bottom of our hearts
In speaking for the boys
America, I say to you
Were your native sons
Believe me it's true
This is your nightmare
on a theatre movie screen
It is your responsibility
To help us fulfill the dream

So, we can be whole
Giving back what we receive
And conquer the distance
from shoulder to sleeve
And conquer the distance
from shoulder to sleeve.....
I speak for the boys
How can this be
I speak for the boys
Who will one day speak for me?

274

Glossary

Adult – A person who has reached full size and strength; fully developed and mature. Antenatal – Having to do with the time a female is pregnant before birth occurs. Also referred to as prenatal.

Approach – A particular way of dealing with a situation, like a new way to problem solve.

Clapback – is a quick, sharp, and often clever response to a criticism or insult.

Capacity – The ability to understand, learn, or comprehend information, like someone's ability to learn a language.

Barriers – Something that blocks or prevents passage, or something that hinders movement or action.

Early Childhood Education – The period of learning and development for children before they begin primary school, typically involving children up to about 8 years of age. It encompasses the instruction, care, and development of young children in specialized settings outside the family.

Engagement – A commitment on the part of the father to participate in programming actively and consistently for their benefit, and the benefit of their child/family.

Family – a group of two or more persons related by birth, marriage, or adoption who live together as a unit.

Father – A father is a male parent who has a child.

Fatherhood – The state of being a father, or the character or authority of a father. Impactful – Having a significant effect or leaving a strong impression, a noticeable and lasting effect.

Intervention – The act of interfering with something to improve it or prevent harm. Involvement – The act of being included in or participating in something, or the state of being engaged in a situation or event. Involvement often implies being a part of an activity, project, or group.

Journey – A focus on the process of getting to a particular place, not necessarily the arrival. It is more about experiences learned along the way.

Juxtapose – To place or deal with close together for a contrasting effect.

Manhood – Refers to the condition of being an adult male, as opposed to boyhood or childhood.

Mother – Female parent; a woman who has borne a child.

Motherhood – The quality or state of being a mother, and it can also refer to the qualities associated with a mother.

Obstacles – That which opposes; anything that stands in the way and hinders progress; obstruction.

Perspective – How an individual thinks about, interprets, and views something, often shaped by their personal experiences, beliefs, and values.

Practitioners – A person who works in or practices a specific profession.

Self-efficacy – Is a person's belief in their own ability to succeed at a particular task or goal It impacts a person's choices, efforts, persistence, and overall performance in various areas of life.

Self-soothing – is a technique to help calm yourself after an upsetting event. It enables the body to return to a normal state after stress.

Service – Labor or duty performed for the benefit of another.

Separation – The act of severing, or disconnecting, or the state of disunion, or disconnection.

Strategies – Carefully planned course of action aimed at achieving a specific goal, often involving the skillful use of resources and tactics.

Street Pharmacist – A drug dealer.

Wraparound – Is a comprehensive strengths-based planning process put in place to respond to a serious mental health or behavioral challenge involving children or youth.

Reflections of A Father
Blog

If you sit quietly and observe an engaged father interacting with his child, it can be awe-inspiring. If they have cultivated their dance based upon a secure base of trust and reciprocity, any observer might gasp. The only way practitioners can experience this or ever get to witness it is if they provide the space for fathers to be themselves. I am not just referring to the physical space within program environments; I am talking about the emotional space, the same emotional space afforded to mothers who are somewhere along the developmental trajectory of parenting but still in need of a lot of guidance and support to grow.

They are not judged! They inspire curiosity and a desire to help. Staff are eager to learn about their past, make sense of it, and help mothers see how it has shaped their present. They are engaged in a process of identifying interests, exploring opportunities, and having conversations about their futures. Futures that involve them and their children.

It has been a few years now since my father died. He was 81 years old, which is a long time to be on this earth. He did not raise me or provide for me. He did not teach me how to grow into manhood. I was fortunate to have other individuals in my life who fulfilled the role.

Today, I evaluate how different my life might have been had he been there. And then I remember it was his absence that instilled in me a desire to be an awesome father. I can laugh now, but I admit I was clueless. How could I provide my children with something that had not been provided for me? I decided to start by committing to just being there from day one, and I tried with all my heart and soul to give, within reason, what I had not received. I was learning along the way, becoming increasingly more comfortable and confident in my capabilities.

I realize I am not very much different than millions of other men who find themselves saddled with the awesome responsibility of having to father a child when they have not been fathered themselves. Yet, in most instances, they do the best they can, drawing upon their own experiences and things they learn along the way. Negotiating unbelievable hurdles and still finding ways to meet with success. However, if you were to ask them whether they are comfortable walking into an early childhood education setting, you would receive a number of different responses.

A small percentage might say yes, some would tell you they are a little leery. Others would tell you that childcare programs are for mothers. For many men, the feeling at least initially has nothing to do with how they have been treated by program staff or the physical space.

It has more to do with their educational history, their level of comfort with the role, how they positioned themselves juxtaposed to their children, and how they define their role. How will they be received, and will they be judged? Many struggle with finding a sense of ease or comfort in settings that have historically been deemed more appropriate for women.

Fathers who are engaged, who love their children, and are not afraid to demonstrate that love find ways to attach, to bond, and build social and emotional relationships with their children. They find comfort in embracing their roles and responsibilities because they know their children in some instances, even better than, some of the mothers we encounter. They too engage in the functional parenting practices that are observable and many more that are not so observable, planning for them, wondering about them, and quietly watching over them as they negotiate developmental trajectories, parenting in ways that cannot be measured.

If we were as curious about fathers as we are about mothers, if we were as thoughtful in our interactions, our communications, our exploratory verbal skills, and our developing and designing support for fathers, they, too, would thrive. Not just as fathers, but as individuals, and as men who love their children and families. With confidence, their competence increases, and they are able to strengthen the social and emotional relationships that drive everything they do when they understand their role, commit to it, and are supported in enhancing their capacity to fulfill that role.

Early childhood educators are in a unique position to support all parents, especially fathers. It begins by being genuine, not patronizing them or over-celebrating their efforts, and by acknowledging and not being afraid to ask them questions about their interactions with their children.

A couple of weeks before my father died, in a telephone conversation, he told me he loved me, and I told him I loved him. Even though he did not raise me. I was able to build a relationship with him because of my children, and for me as well.

The ambivalence is deep within me, and sometimes it surfaces to the top, and I am confronted with unresolved feelings. I have to wrestle with the fact that he failed me by not being there, by not providing for me, and by not laying the groundwork for me to develop a healthy sense of self.

Fortunately, my mother was a loving individual, and I am whole because of my relationship with her; yet, there is a void when it comes to my father. It took a long time to fully understand me because I did not know him. Still, I advocate daily for fathers and mothers to have equal say and an equal place at the table when it comes to their children.

Head Start programs are in a prime position to create welcoming environments, contributing to a Culture of Inclusion, and establishing meaningful relationships with fathers so that all parents feel welcome. Within your respective spaces, I ask that you extend yourselves a little more, finding ways to engage and build stronger relationships with fathers across the Head Start universe, for their sake and for the sake of their children.

References

Auerbach, C. F., Hayes, D., Jones, D., & Silverstein, L. B. (n.d.). In their own words: Early Head Start fathers.

Beitel, A., & Parke, R. (1998). Paternal involvement in infancy: The role of maternal and paternal attitudes. *Journal of Family Psychology*, 12, 268-288.

Blumenthal, S. (2012). *Violence as communication* (pp. 5-7).

Cochran, D. (1997). African American fathers: A decade review of the literature. *Families in Society*, 78(4), 340-350.

Cormick, C., & Kennedy, J. (1994). Parent-child attachment working models and self-esteem in adolescence. *Journal of Youth and Adolescence*, 23, 1-18.

Danziger, S., & Radin, N. (1990). Absent does not equal uninvolved: Predictors of fathering in teen mother families. *Journal of Marriage and the Family*, 52, 636-642.

Hendricks, L. E. (1988). Outreach with teenage fathers: A preliminary report on three ethnic groups. *Adolescence*, 23(91), 711-720.

Hendricks, L. E., & Solomon, A. M. (1987). Reaching Black male adolescent parents through nontraditional techniques. *Child & Youth Services*, 9(1), 111-124.

Jones, D. (2000). Father absence paradigm: A comparative study of African American father absence within the family and gender/role prescription as an explanation. [Unpublished manuscript].

Jones, D., Spriggs, A. L., & Waliser, M. N. E. (2005). From theory to practice: An evidence-based model of father engagement in early childhood programs.

Kiselica, M. S. (1996). Parenting skills training with teenage fathers. In M. P. Andronico (Ed.), *Men in groups: Insights, interventions, and psychoeducational work* (pp. 283-300). American Psychological Association.

Lamb, M. E. (1975). Fathers: Forgotten contributors to child development. *Human Development*, 18, 245-266.

Lamb, M. E. (1997). The development of father-infant relationships. In M. E. Lamb (Ed.), *The role of the father in child development* (3rd ed., pp. 104-120). Wiley.

Miller, D. B. (1994). Influences on parental involvement of African American adolescent fathers. *Child and Adolescent Social Work Journal*, 11(5), 363-378.

Parke, R. D. (1995). Fathers and families. In M. H. Bornstein (Ed.), *Handbook of parenting: Volume 3 status and social conditions of parenting* (pp. 27-64). Lawrence Erlbaum Associates.

Rhein, L. M., Ginsburg, K. R., Schwartz, D. F., Pinto-Martin, J. A., Zhao, H., Morgan, A. P., Alexander, S. E., & Slap, G. B. (1997). Teen father participation in child rearing: Family perspectives. *Journal of Adolescent Health*, 21(4), 244-252.

Roggman, L. A., Boyce, L. K., Cook, G. A., & Cook, J. (2002). Getting dads involved: Predictors of father involvement in Early Head Start and with their children. *Infant Mental Health*, 23(1-2), 1962-1978.

Stone, G., & McKenry, P. (1998). Nonresidential father involvement: A test of mid-range theory. *Journal of Genetic Psychology*, 159, 313-336.

Summers, J. A., Raikes, H., Butler, J., Spicer, P., Pan, B., Shaw, S., Johnson, M., McAllister, C., & Johnson, D. (1999). Low-income fathers' and mothers' perceptions of the father role: A qualitative study in four early head start communities. *Infant Mental Health Journal*, 20(3), 291-304.